making it right

product management for a startup world

Imprint

Published 2014 by Smashing Magazine GmbH, Freiburg, Germany.
ISBN: 9781502322401 .
Cover Design: Francisco Inchauste.
Chapter Illustrations: Anna Shuvalova.
Technical Editing: Francisco Inchauste.
Copyediting and Proofreading: Owen Gregory.
Editing and Quality Control: Vitaly Friedman.
eBook Production: Cosima Mielke.

Making It Right: Product Management For A Startup World was written by
Rian van der Merwe.

For Jessica, Aralyn, and Emery. Home is where you are.

TABLE OF CONTENTS

Part 1: Introduction

Introduction

On February 9, 2010 Google's vice president of product management, Bradley Horowitz, got on stage at a press conference to introduce a product called Google Buzz. Hailed as "a new way to start conversations about the things you find interesting[1]", Buzz was a social network that lived inside Gmail[2] and promised features like a "rich, fast sharing experience", and a relevancy filter to highlight only the most important items.

Unfortunately Google didn't have much time to bask in the glory of the new social network's release. Almost immediately, a feature intended to save users time turned into a nightmare for the company. Once a user opted in to Google Buzz, they immediately auto-followed everyone they emailed or chatted with frequently. The bigger problem was that this information was also made available on the user's public Google profile, meaning anyone could see whom they contacted most frequently. By delivering on its "no setup required!" promise, Google inadvertently stepped into a privacy controversy from which the product never fully recovered.

On February 10 — a day after the launch — headlines like "Google Buzz: Privacy nightmare[3]" and "WARNING: Google Buzz Has A Huge Privacy Flaw[4]" started to appear on popular technology blogs. The articles aimed to edu-

---

1. "Introducing Google Buzz" – http://smashed.by/buzz
2. Google Gmail press conference – http://smashed.by/buzz-release
3. "Google Buzz: Privacy nightmare" – http://smashed.by/nightmare
4. "WARNING: Google Buzz Has A Huge Privacy Flaw" – http://smashed.by/privacy-flaw

cate users about aspects of Buzz that the interface failed to explain in a satisfactory manner: how a user's information was displayed publicly; how to make the information private; and how to edit the list of people they followed.

The Google Buzz team reacted immediately and worked around the clock to address the issues. On February 11 Google released a feature to make it easier for users not to show the list of people they followed on their public Google profiles. But it still auto-followed everyone they emailed and chatted with regularly. So the bad press kept coming. On February 12 Business Insider published a photo of a masked Eminem wielding a chain saw beneath the headline "Outraged Blogger Is Automatically Being Followed By Her Abusive Ex-Husband On Google Buzz[5]".

Things were not going well for the Google Buzz team.

But the only way out was through, so they pushed ahead, setting up a dedicated war room and pushing Google Buzz into "Code Red[6]" so that updates could be released as soon as possible.

On February 14 the team announced a bunch of changes to Buzz[7], including the big one: Buzz would no longer auto-follow users during setup. Instead, Buzz would change to an auto-suggest model, meaning users would have to explicitly select the people they want to follow. However, for some it was too little, too late. On

---

5. "Outraged Blogger Is Automatically Being Followed By Her Abusive Ex-Husband On Google Buzz" – http://smashed.by/stalking
6. "How Google Went Into 'Code Red' And Saved Google Buzz" – http://smashed.by/code-red
7. "A new Buzz start-up experience based on your feedback" – http://smashed.by/buzz-feedback

February 16 a complaint about the privacy issues was filed against Google with the Federal Trade Commission[8]. A Harvard Law School student filed a class action law suit against the company on the same day.

Outraged Blogger Is Automatically Being Followed By Her Abusive Ex-Husband On Google Buzz

Nick Saint | Feb. 12, 2010, 11:31 AM | 🔺 10,502 | 💬 57

🅕 Recommend 31   in Share 1   🐦 Tweet 4   ℜ +1 5   ✉ Email   More

The glaring privacy flaws in Google Buzz, which the company has failed to address fully, have hit home for one blogger who says she is now being auto-followed by her abusive ex-husband and his friends.

Harriet Jacobs (a name she goes by) writes on her blog that the people she receives email from most often include her ex-husband, his friends, and abusive commenters.

AP

The tech press got some great headlines out of the Google Buzz story (Source: Business Insider[9])

Still, slowly but surely, the chaos subsided. Eventually the tech press moved on to the next juicy story, and Google Buzz chugged along for a while. Of course, the story of Google Buzz didn't have a happy ending. On December 15,

---

8. The FTC complaint was settled on March 30, 2011. Read the press release here: http://smashed.by/ftc
9. "Outraged Blogger Is Automatically Being Followed By Her Abusive Ex-Husband On Google Buzz" – http://smashed.by/stalking

2011 both Google Buzz and the Buzz API shut down for all users, so the company could focus on its Google+ social network instead.

What does Google Buzz have to do with this book? Well, this is a book about product management and how to build successful products. And if you just read this story and said to yourself, "Hey, that sounds like a fun experience to be part of!", then product management is almost certainly the career for you. If you wanted to hide under your desk and have a stiff drink, it's probably best to consider a different career path. Because behind every decision, every mistake, every solution, and every code release on Google Buzz there was a product manager who took responsibility for every consequence. During the run-up to the launch, the first few chaotic days, as well as the ensuing battle to convince people to use the product, a product manager stood in the gap between the product and the market to provide long-term vision, as well as tactical direction to keep things moving forward.

Product management is one of the most exhausting, exhilarating, stressful, and rewarding careers out there. It's not for the faint of heart. It's for people who want to move mountains. It swallows some whole, but others derive endless invigoration and passion from the pace and the impact and the glory and the huge potential for failure as well as success. There's no other job like it, and this is a book to help you make it *your* job.

I fear I may have not sold the role of product management very well by jumping in with a story about Google Buzz. There's nothing like a dose of reality to wake us up to what being a product manager is about: a boundless tenacity to build the best products in the world. Yet, to balance things out, let's consider a different story — the app, Clear[10] from Realmac Software.

I can only imagine the miles and miles of chaotic complexity that product managers, designers, and developers had to wade through to arrive at the simplicity of Clear – a to-do list app for the iPhone and Mac. The first time I used the app, Rebekah Cox's definition of design[11] kept popping into my head:

> Design is a set of decisions about a product. It's not an interface or an aesthetic, it's not a brand or a color. Design is the actual decisions.

And Realmac made some difficult decisions that resulted in a great product. I can picture the endless, difficult meetings and arguments that must have happened to decide what features to include in the app. Should we have projects and contexts? No. How about due dates and filters? Nope. Well, why not!? Because Clear is a prioritized list of tasks that is fast and easy to edit. That's it. Nothing less, nothing more.

To understand the beauty of Clear, it's not just important to look at what it is, but also what it's not. Clear is a great way to view and prioritize a simple list of tasks, but it's not a replacement for hardcore task management systems, like Omnifocus. But Omnifocus is overkill for sim-

10. Clear from Realmac Software – http://smashed.by/clear
11. Web 2.0 Expo Presentation – http://smashed.by/web-expo

ple tasks like making a car appointment or getting coffee at the store. And that is the gap that Clear fills.

Clear is focused on two things that make it superior to other similar apps:

- **Speed**: it's really fast. When it starts up you can instantly start typing. This is crucial to quickly capture that all-important thing you don't want to forget.

- **Effortless editing**: it's completely gesture-based — no chrome, no fluff, no fancy visual design. You tap, you type, you swipe, you close. These gestures are easy to learn and intuitive.

It's really hard to resist the temptation to build an app that tries to solve every problem for every person in the world. What makes the product management on Clear so impressive is that they walked through the fire of saying no to potentially great features, and emerged on the other side probably scorched and battered, but also with a great app for listing tasks and editing them quickly. Want more in your to-do list app? That's what Omnifocus is for. And they're OK with that. That's something to be proud of.

The juxtaposed stories of Google Buzz and Clear hopefully show us that even though product management is not always an easy job, it's also never a boring one.

When I started out in product management I read a bunch of books about it, but none prepared me for the realities I would face once I got stuck in. A big problem is that the role goes by many different names — and if that's not reason enough to be confused, some companies define product manager completely differently from how it's understood elsewhere. So you have program managers, project managers, and business analysts sometimes fulfilling the role of product manager. And then you have product managers in roles that could more accurately be called production managers or product owners. I know we sometimes get stuck in our quest to Define The Damn Thing, but in the case of product management, it's effort well spent, because it's quite the jungle out there.

So with that as background, I set out to write this book to accomplish three goals:

1. Define the roles and responsibilities of product managers in the software development context. There are so many people building digital products and doing a bunch of things that can be defined as product management, but what is lacking is a holistic definition of and a systematic approach to the role. I hope to fill that gap with this book.

2. Explain why product management is an essential role in any organization, and what characteristics managers should look for when they hire product managers.

3. Provide a framework and practical guidance for strategic product management; a framework that details the elements of product planning and product execution that make up a product manager's day-to-day work.

That's how this book came to be, and how it's structured.

In Part 1 I'll give an overview of the product manager role. What it's like, who it's for, why it's important, and how it fits into an organization.

In Part 2 I'll discuss the elements of product planning. How to decide what to build, how to prioritize the needs of different customers and stakeholders, and how to turn that into a strategic product plan and roadmap for delivery.

In Part 3 I'll discuss how to make the strategy real through product execution. This is where we'll get into the nitty-gritty of product definition, hypothesis testing, design, and release cycles.

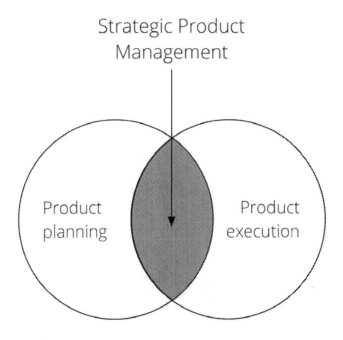

Strategic product management

This book is for anyone considering a career in product management, or those who have been in the field for a while and are looking for a more formal framework for the work they do. Most of us come to product management from different circumstances; design, business analysis, and development backgrounds are the most common. So this is also a book for those who want to keep working in their chosen specializations, but would like to gain a better understanding of how their work fits into the bigger picture of product strategy and delivery.

On a personal level, this book is about more than strategies, processes, and methodologies. We live in an amazing time dominated not by consumers, but by people who create software. Because of the internet and advances in digital technology we have broad access to the tools and expertise needed to create new products and improve existing ones. And I want to be part of that movement. I want to do what I can to contribute, and help foster that passion to create in others. My fear — and why I believe the ideas in this book are so important — is that we lack the patience and the frameworks required to make sure we understand users before we start building products for them. We lack the appropriate tools to properly plan and execute our product ideas. And, most of all, we still lack the broad adoption of teams of people who obsess over these things in our organizations — the product, its users, and how to make both successful.

My desire is that this book would empower product managers to build better products. I'll provide a structured framework — with just the right amount of process — to make product managers confident that they are building the right products, at the right time, for the right people.

I hope that anyone who works to make software, websites, or mobile applications will find this book useful to build products that are meaningful to users, and that are sustainable as businesses.

Let's get started. ❧

CHAPTER 1:

Roles And Responsibilities Of The Product Manager

What is a product manager, and what do they do every day? Good question.

The first confusion we have to clear up is what we mean by the word *product*. In the context of software development, the product is the website, application, or online service that users interact with. Depending on the size of the company and its products, a product manager can be responsible for an entire system (like a mobile app), or only part of a system (like the checkout flow on an e-commerce site, across all devices).

This is confusing because in most contexts a product is a thing you sell to people. Particularly in the context of e-commerce, product management often gets confused with category management: the team that deals with sourcing and merchandising the products sold on an e-commerce site. So, yes, product probably isn't the best word for it. But it's what we have, and the definition we'll use to explore this role.

To get to a definition of the product management role, let's start by looking at Marc Andreessen's view of the only thing that matters in a startup environment[12] (my emphasis added in bold):

---

12. "Product/Market Fit" – http://smashed.by/market-fit

The quality of a startup's product can be defined as how impressive the product is to one customer or user who actually uses it: How easy is the product to use? How feature rich is it? How fast is it? How extensible is it? How polished is it? How many (or rather, how few) bugs does it have?

The size of a startup's market is the number, and growth rate, of those customers or users for that product.

[...]

The only thing that matters is getting to product/market fit. **Product/market fit means being in a good market with a product that can satisfy that market.**

Even though Marc wrote this specifically for the startup context, the importance of product/market fit has universal truth in any organization — whether that organization is getting a new product into the market, or redesigning an existing experience, or anything in between. It is a universal roadmap for success, and the core of what product managers are responsible for.

With that as backdrop, my definition of the role of product manager is as follows:

The product manager's mission is to achieve business success by meeting user needs through the continuous planning and execution of digital product solutions.

This definition summarizes all the things that product managers need to obsess over: the target market; the intricacies of the product; what the business needs to achieve success; and how to measure that success. It further encapsulates the three things that product managers should never lose sight of:

- The ultimate measure of success is the health of the business, and therefore the value that the product provides to users.

- Everything starts with a good understanding of the target market and its needs, so that the focus remains on the quality of the product experience.

- A continuous cycle of planning and execution is required to meet these market needs in a way that is sustainable.

So how does this translate to what product managers do every day? That is, of course, what this book is about. By way of introduction, Marty Cagan has a great list of common tasks that product managers are responsible for in his ebook *Behind Every Great Product*[13]. The list includes:

- Identifying and assessing the validity and feasibility of product opportunities.

- Making sure the right product is delivered at the right time.

- Developing the product strategy and roadmap for development.

---

13. *Behind Every Great Product* – http://smashed.by/product-manager

- Leading the team in the execution of the product roadmap.

- Evangelizing the product internally to the executive team, and colleagues.

- Representing customers through the product development process.

We'll spend many chapters discussing each of these activities — and more. But before we get to that, we need to answer a few important questions. First, do companies really need product managers? And if we can agree on that, what are the characteristics of a good product manager? Also, where does this role fit into the organizational structure? Let's explore these questions.

Why Companies Need Product Managers

Product management can be a hard sell for some companies. Common objections to the role include:

- "We have different people in the organization who fulfill each of these functions as part of their roles."

- "I don't see how the role will make us more money."

- "Product managers will just slow us down."

- "I don't want to relinquish control of the product to someone else." (OK, that one is usually thought without being said out loud.)

These appear to be valid concerns at first, but only if the role is not well understood — or if there are bad product managers in the organization who perpetuate these perceptions.

The truth is that, to be effective, the product management role for a particular product or area can't be fulfilled by multiple people. It is essential for the product manager to see the whole picture — the strategic vision as well as the implementation details — to help them make good decisions about the product. If the knowledge of different parts of the process is in the heads of different people, the holistic view goes away, taking all the value out of the role.

Let's look at two major benefits of product management.

PRODUCT MANAGERS ENSURE A MARKET-DRIVEN APPROACH

The key argument in favor of product management is that it helps companies to be driven by the needs and goals of their target market, not the forces of technology or fad. And, as Barbara Nelson puts it in "Who Needs Product Management?[14]":

> It is vastly easier to identify market problems and solve them with technology than it is to find buyers for your existing technology.

---

14. "Who Needs Product Management?" – http://smashed.by/pmanagement

If done right, being market-driven results in long-term, sustainable, profitable businesses, because the company remains focused on solving market problems as opposed to looking for things to do with the latest technologies. Being market-driven is important because such companies are proven to be more profitable than those driven by other factors (31% more profitable, according to research[15]).

This doesn't mean that you only focus on incremental change in lieu of product innovation. Identifying market problems isn't just about finding existing issues to improve (for example, "60% of users drop off on this page, so let's fix that"), but also about creating new products to satisfy unmet needs ("Cell phones suck, let's make a better one"). One of the things we'll discuss later on is how to do research that uncovers the needs behind the features, to assist companies with both innovation and iteration.

PRODUCT MANAGERS IMPROVE TIME-TO-EVERYTHING

The second major benefit of product management is that it reduces the time it takes to reach the organization's goals. A well-defined and appropriate product development process run by effective product managers improves both time-to-market as well as time-to-revenue.

The reason for faster turnaround times is that product managers are responsible for figuring out what's worth

---

15. "Managerial Representations of Competitive Advantage," George S. Day and Prakash Nedungadi, *Journal of Marketing 58* (April 1994): 40.

building, and what is not. This means that less time is spent on the spaghetti approach to product development (throwing things against the wall to see what sticks), and more time is spent on building products that have been validated in the market. This approach also provides focus to an organization, so it's able to dedicate more people to products that are likely to succeed, as opposed to spreading people too thin on projects that no one is sure will reach product/market fit.

Characteristics Of A Good Product Manager

Now that we've covered the importance of product management, the next question is, "Who are these people?"

Most of us are familiar with the idea of T-shaped people: those who have deep knowledge in one or two areas, combined with a reasonable understanding of a variety of disciplines related to their main field of focus. In 2009 Bill Buxton wrote an interesting article for Businessweek in which he calls for more "I-shaped" people[16]:

> These have their feet firmly planted in the mud of the practical world, and yet stretch far enough to stick their head in the clouds when they need to. Furthermore, they simultaneously span all of the space in between.

This is a good description of the unique blend of skills that product managers (PMs) need. First, they need to

---

16. "Innovation Calls For I-Shaped People" – http://smashed.by/ishape

have their heads in the clouds. PMs need to be leaders who can look into the future and think strategically. They need to be able to develop a vision for where a product should go — and they need to be able to communicate that vision effectively. Further, PMs need to show their teams how they plan to get to that vision. And I do mean show — through sketches, prototypes, storyboards, or whatever it takes to get the message across. Good PMs are also able to remain flexible and change course when needed, perhaps when there is a big shift in market needs or expectations, or a great business opportunity presents itself.

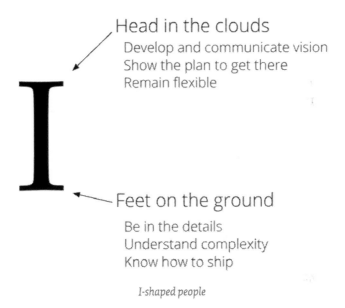

Head in the clouds
Develop and communicate vision
Show the plan to get there
Remain flexible

Feet on the ground
Be in the details
Understand complexity
Know how to ship

I-shaped people

But good PMs also have their feet on the ground. They pay attention to detail, and they know their products inside out. They are the product's biggest users — and its biggest fans and critics. They understand every aspect of the complexity that needs to be worked through in each product decision. And they're able to make those decisions quickly based on all the information they have at their disposal.

Most importantly, PMs know how to ship. They know how to execute and rally a team to get products and improvements out in the world where the target market can use them and provide feedback.

In short, PMs are visionaries as well as doers. Managers as well as makers. And they need to move seamlessly between those extremes, sometimes at a moment's notice. Sound difficult? That's only the beginning. Let's look at some more characteristics of good product managers:

- Leader and collaborator

- Communicator and negotiator

- Passionate and empathic

- Qualified and curious

- Trustworthy and ethical

- Responsible and flexible

LEADER AND COLLABORATOR

Being a leader and a collaborator at the same time can be a difficult balance to strike. The first challenge is that collaboration is often mistaken for consensus. But that's not the case. Consensus cultures often produce watered down, unexciting products. Products where endless rounds of give-and-take have worn down the original idea to a shadow of what it once was. Consensus cultures also wear down the teams working on the product, because no one really gets what they want, they just get some of it.

Collaboration is different. In collaboration cultures people understand that even though everyone gets a voice, not everyone gets to decide. People are able to air their opinions, argue passionately for how they believe things should be done, and try to negotiate compromises. But it certainly doesn't mean that everyone has to agree with every decision.

The first step to building a collaboration culture is being a good leader. As you've probably surmised by now, the product manager is the ultimate decision-maker. But that only works if they are a trusted and respected leader in the organization — someone who can get teams excited about a vision, as well as make the best decisions for the benefit of the company and its customers. Good leaders also readily admit when they make a wrong decision, and they own up to it and do whatever they can to fix the mistake.

This isn't a book about leadership — there are plenty of those to go around. But I'll still share one piece of leadership advice from French writer and aviator Antoine de Saint Exupéry[17] that has helped me over the years:

---

17. A loose English paraphrase of Antoine de Saint Exupéry's French poem *Dessine-moi un bateau* (Make me a boat), found in *Citadelle* (1948) – http://smashed.by/makemeaboat

If you want to build a ship, don't drum people up togeth-
er to collect wood, and don't assign them tasks and
work. Rather teach them to long for the endless immen-
sity of the sea.

What does "the endless immensity of the sea" mean in
your context? Instead of telling people to build a bunch of
features, how can you inspire them to think about how
the product will help users accomplish their goals? That's
how you'll be able to unite teams around a common vision.

So, how does a good leader foster this kind of collaboration culture? By creating the right environment and
processes that allow collaboration to feed on itself, and
understanding that every person is different and will react unpredictably at some point.

To create the right environment and processes for collaboration, focus on the physical environment first. Make
sure that physical work spaces allow both for impromptu
discussions with team members, as well as the ability to
shut everyone else out and work free of distractions for a
period of time. The MailChimp office is a great example
of this. The team created a collaborative work space[18]
based on the following principles:

- **Commingle and cross-pollinate.** Instead of segregating
  teams, mix people up based on personalities and the projects they're working on. This leads to valuable discus-

---

18. "New MailChimp: Collaboration by Design" – http://smashed.by/
collaborationbydesign

sions that might not have happened if everyone is stuck in their own silos.

- **Facilitate movement.** Open desks, couches, standing tables: these are all ways to encourage people to move around and work together when needed.

- **Ideas everywhere.** Cover walls and whiteboards with sketches, designs, prioritization lists, roadmaps. This not only contributes to better communication, but also leaves the door open for anyone to improve the ideas people are working on.

- **Create convergence.** A common space for lunch (and coffee!) is important because it facilitates people running into each other, even if they don't normally work together on a project. This, again, can result in great ideas and perspectives.

- **Create retreats.** The hustle and bustle of collaboration spaces has great energy, but can sometimes be distracting. Occasionally individuals or teams need a quiet space to work, so make sure there are meeting rooms or quiet retreats where there won't be any interruptions.

Work spaces are more important than we might think. We've gone to great lengths to try to create a welcoming, creative space at the studio I used to work at, and we see it paying off. Most clients prefer to come to us when we're having meetings, and they cite two reasons: excellent coffee (we went a little overboard on the coffee), and a great atmosphere to work in.

Steve Jobs understood the value of physical spaces very well. He had this to say about the design of Pixar's new campus[19]:

> *If a building doesn't encourage [collaboration], you'll lose a lot of innovation and the magic that's sparked by serendipity. So we designed the building to make people get out of their offices and mingle in the central atrium with people they might not otherwise see.*

Of course, physical space is only one part of the equation. A lot of work happens remotely now, and we have enough tools at our disposal to make that an effective and rewarding experience for everyone involved. From communication tools like Campfire, HipChat, and Slack, to collaborative project management tools like Trello, Basecamp, and Jira, to source code repositories like GitHub and Bitbucket, there's no excuse anymore to force everyone to be in the same physical space at all times. There is still much value in talking to people face to face, and collaborating in certain areas of the process, but even that can happen in digital spaces.

So, what's next after you've worked on the physical and digital environments? A feared word... Many people hear "process" and think it's synonymous with "things I have to do instead of working". But we're going to talk a lot about appropriate, or right-fidelity processes in this book. To quote Michael Lopp: "Engineers don't hate process. They hate process that can't defend itself[20]."

---

19. Isaacson, Walter: *Steve Jobs.*

When it comes to creating a culture of collaboration, there are several processes that can make life easier for the whole team — defendable processes.

One essential collaboration process to get right is regular feedback sessions on design, development, and business decisions. The problem is that feedback sessions can get out of hand quickly, because we're just not very good at providing (or receiving) feedback. We are prone to seeing the negative parts of someone's ideas first, so we often jump straight into the teardown. This puts the person on the receiving end in defensive mode right away, which usually starts a negative spiral into unhelpful arguments and distrust.

There is, however, a better way. In an interview on criticism and judgment, French philosopher Michel Foucault once laid out the purpose of any good critique[21]. In his view, criticism should be focused not on what doesn't work, but on how you can build on the ideas of others to make it better:

> I can't help but dream about a kind of criticism that
> would try not to judge but to bring an oeuvre, a book, a
> sentence, an idea to life; it would fight fires, watch grass
> grow, listen to the wind, and catch the sea foam in the
> breeze and scatter it. It would multiply not judgements
> but signs of existence; it would summon them, drag
> them from their sleep. Perhaps it would invent them

20. "The Process Myth" – http://smashed.by/process-myth
21. *Politics, Philosophy, Culture: Interviews and Other Writings, 1977–1984*, Michel Foucault. (http://smashed.by/foucault)

sometimes — all the better. Criticism that hands down sentences sends me to sleep; I'd like a criticism of scintillating leaps of the imagination. It would not be sovereign or dressed in red. It would bear the lightning of possible storms.

Keeping this purpose in mind, I particularly like the process used by Jared Spool and his team at UIE[22]. The team uses this specifically for design critiques, but it can be applied generically to any kind of feedback session. Here's how the process works:

- The person presenting their idea or work describes the problem they are trying to solve.

- If everyone agrees on the problem, the team moves on. However, if there isn't agreement on the problem that is being solved, some discussion is needed to clarify. Hopefully this step isn't needed, though.

- Next, the presenter communicates their idea or shows their work to the team. The goal is not only to show the finished product, but to explain the thought process behind the idea or deliverable. The presenter should remain focused on how the idea will solve the problem that everyone agreed on.

- The first step for feedback is for the people in the room to point out what they like about the idea. This isn't a gimmick to set up the crap sandwich method (you know:

---

22. "Moving from Critical Review to Critique" – http://smashed.by/critical-review

start and end with something positive, eviscerate in the middle). Instead, this step helps to highlight what direction is desirable as a solution to the problem.

- Critique follows as the next step, not as direct attacks or phrases such as "I don't like…", but as questions about the idea. Team members ask if a different solution was considered, what the reason was for a particular choice, and so on. This gives the presenter a chance to respond if they've thought through the issue already, or else, make a note to address the issue for the next iteration.

- At the end of the meeting, the team reviews the notes, especially what everyone liked, and what questions they had. The presenter then goes away to work on the next iteration of the idea.

As the product manager you are responsible for making sure feedback sessions happen, and that they are respectful and useful. Scott Berkun has a great set of ground rules about critiques[23] that are worth remembering:

- **Take control of the feedback process.** Feedback is something that you should make happen, because that's how it happens on your terms and in a way that improves the product. If you just wait for feedback to happen to you, it's going to happen in meetings when you're not prepared, you'll be on the defensive, and the focus will shift off product to politics.

23. "How to give and receive criticism" – http://smashed.by/berkun

- **Pick your partners.** Some people are better at giving feedback than others. Find feedback partners who have the relevant experience you need to make the product better.

- **Strive to hear it all, informally and early.** Don't wait until the product is nearly finished before you get feedback. Discuss ideas, concepts, and sketches way before you discuss comps and working code.

The goal of collaboration is for ideas to become better by building on the best parts of different thoughts and viewpoints. As long as people trust that the decision-maker (that's you, dear product manager) has the product's and the company's best interests at heart, they won't have a problem with not getting their way every once in a while. Be confident, trustworthy, and decisive — and make sure everyone feels comfortable to raise their opinions with the team. The book *Crucial Conversations: Tools for Talking When Stakes Are High*[24] is a great resource on how to build this type of environment.

One final note on collaboration. The design and strategy firm Cooper has a great set of guiding principles to ensure good collaboration within and across teams[25]. Some of those guidelines — once again adjusted for a broader context than just design — are:

---

24. *Crucial Conversations: Tools for Talking When Stakes Are High*, Kerry Patterson, Joseph Grenny, Ron McMillan and Al Switzler. (http://smashed.by/amzn-1)
25. "Better together; the practice of successful creative collaboration" – http://smashed.by/better-together

- **Don't work alone.** There needs to be a natural ebb and flow to the way teams work. Some work is going to be done by individuals on their own (documentation, Photoshop comp creation, and so on), but that period of working alone should always be followed by time together as a team to provide critique and push ideas forward.

- **Externalize thinking.** It's important to share early iterations of an idea with the team. We'll discuss this in detail later, but once a team starts iterating on an idea, it becomes much harder to change course. Talking about early stage ideas helps the team consider a variety of alternatives.

- **Presume value, even when it's not obvious.** This is the "Yes, and…" trick they teach us in brainstorming classes. Instead of finding fault with something, try to find ways you can build on the ideas that are shared.

- **Leave egos at the door.** This is often the most difficult component of collaboration, but the most essential one. It's not just important to give good feedback, it's also essential to receive it well. Being good at receiving feedback means listening intently, writing things down, requesting more details where needed, and most of all, having enough humility to assume that you're going to be wrong about things every once in a while. It's much better to fix mistakes early in the development process than it is to fight for your point and have it fail once it's live. Leaving egos at the door means everyone gets to look good, because you're less likely to make mistakes.

All of this is much easier said than done, of course. Product managers need to steer the team through the collaboration process. And sometimes the trust just won't be there in the beginning. That's OK — trust takes time. Live these values, lead by example, and the culture will come.

COMMUNICATOR AND NEGOTIATOR

A more accurate label for this section may be "Overcommunicator and Negotiator," because if there's one thing a product manager can never get tired of, it's telling people what's going on. But instead of sending tons of email, a better way — and something we'll discuss quite a bit — is to work out in the open as much as possible. Make sure that notes, sketches, plans, and strategies are all accessible to everyone inside the company at all times. This can be either on whiteboards across the office, or in company wikis or project spaces. Working in public has the added benefit of contextual conversations: all comments and decisions are in one place, as opposed to spread out over multiple emails (or worse, in meetings where no one remembered to take notes...).

Being a product manager can sometimes feel like being torn limb from limb. Most stakeholders only have their own department's interests at heart (as they should — they're paid to fight the good fight for what they care about). In contrast, the product manager needs to negotiate the best solution out of all the different directions that stakeholders want to take, and then communicate the decisions effectively and without alienating the people who don't get their way. That's not an easy job.

What product management sometimes feels like (central panel of Martyrdom of St Hippolyte triptych by Dieric Bouts, c1468)

The phrase the design community has adopted to refer to the difficult process of managing the expectations (and assertions) of a variety of stakeholders is: design by committee. Once again, a more generic decisions-by-committee culture is often pervasive, particularly in large organizations. I've always liked the approach Speider Schneider proposes in his article "Why Design-By-Committee Should Die[26]":

---

26. "Why Design-By-Committee Should Die" – http://smashed.by/design-committees

The sensible answer is to listen, absorb, discuss, be able to defend any design decision with clarity and reason, know when to pick your battles and know when to let go.

This is not as easy as it sounds, so over time I've developed the following guidelines to deal with the decisions by committee in a systematic way.

Respond to every piece of feedback

It takes time to respond to every demand, criticism, question, and idea. But failing to respond will waste even more time and energy down the road. It's one thing when someone listens to your idea and doesn't use it. It's something else entirely when someone doesn't even listen. Instead of dealing with the political ramifications of not hearing people out, take the time to respond thoughtfully whenever someone gives feedback (no matter how invalid) or sends an idea along.

Note what feedback is being incorporated

When you implement a good idea, don't just do it quietly. It's an opportunity to show that you're flexible and open to good feedback. So let people know when and how their ideas are being used. Also, this should go without saying, but don't take credit for someone else's ideas.

When feedback is not being incorporated, explain why

Practically speaking, most of the feedback you receive won't be incorporated into the product. It's important not to sweep those decisions under the rug. By forcing yourself to be clear and upfront about feedback that isn't incorporated, you'll also force yourself to think through the decision and defend it properly. Sometimes you'll even realize that what you initially dismissed as a bad idea would be an improvement after all. The main benefit of doing this is that people are generally OK with it if their feedback isn't being used, as long as they've been heard, and there's a good reason for the decision.

Use a validation stack to defend decisions

In their book *Undercover User Experience Design*[27] Cennydd Bowles and James Box explain the user experience validation stack, a method that can, once again, be applied generically to defend product decision. When defending a decision, always try to use evidence in the form of data collected directly from users, such as usability testing, or web analytics. If you don't have direct user data, look for third-party research — either previous research you've done, or research in similar areas that are applicable to the problems you are trying to solve. If all else fails, fall back on theory. The principles of visual perception, persuasion, psychology, and so on come in very handy to explain why you've made certain decisions.

These guidelines should make it easier to negotiate different needs and requests from internal stakeholders. But remember Speider's recommendation in his article: you

---

27. *Undercover User Experience Design*, Cennydd Bowles and James Box. (http://undercoverux.com/)

must know when to pick your battles, and know when to let go. That's the art of being a good negotiator and communicator.

PASSIONATE AND EMPATHIC

Product managers have a love and deep respect for well-designed, well-made products — physical as well as digital. And they live to create products like that. They are the people who go to parties and can't shut up about a new site or app they saw recently; or more likely, they can't shut up about what they're working on and how cool it is.

But they're not just passionate about the product: they're passionate about the people who use the products as well. They have a very good understanding of their market — their customers' values, priorities, perceptions, and experiences. Passion for a product is useless without empathy — a deep care and understanding — about the people who use the product. I don't think it's possible to build great products without the ability to get into the minds of the people who use the product. If we want to anticipate what people want to do, and guide them along that path, empathy is non-negotiable.

QUALIFIED AND CURIOUS

Product managers usually come from specialist backgrounds like user experience design, programming, or business analysis. In order to apply the knowledge from their fields more generally — in other words, becoming more I-shaped — they not only need to be extremely comfortable in their current skill sets, but they must also be able to learn new skills very quickly (and under great pressure). This combination of being qualified as well as able to keep learning indicates that product managers need to be insatiably curious in everything they do. Why? Cap Watkins puts it really well[28]:

> [...]if you're intensely curious, I tend to worry less about those other skills. Over and over I watch great designers acquire new skills and push the boundaries of what can be done through sheer curiosity and force of will. Curiosity forces us to stay up all night teaching ourselves a new Photoshop technique. It wakes us up in the middle of the night because it can't let go of the interaction problem we haven't nailed yet. I honestly think it's the single, most important trait a designer (or, hell, anyone working in tech) can possess.

Good product managers do whatever it takes to make the product successful. They constantly worry about the tiniest of details as well as the biggest of strategy questions. And instead of being overwhelmed by the sheer amount of what needs to be done, their curiosity pushes them to remain committed and become as qualified as possible to make the right decisions.

TRUSTWORTHY AND ETHICAL

Good product managers build trust with their teams with every decision they make. To be trustworthy, PMs need to be fair (more on this a bit later), consistent, and always

---

28. "Curiosity Required" – http://smashed.by/curiosity

take responsibility for their decisions. They also have to admit when they're wrong, which can be very difficult at the best of times.

At one extreme, PMs need to be confident about the decisions they make. They need to keep learning and growing, and hone their craft constantly. Solid theory and excellent technique need to become so ingrained that they simply become second nature, cornerstones of everything they do.

But equally important, they need to be open to the possibility that some of their decisions might be wrong. In fact, they need to welcome it. They should hang on to a measure of self-doubt every time they present a new solution to the team or the world. Admitting that someone else's ideas are better than your own, and making changes based on good critique do wonders to improve products — and build trust within the team. In the design context John Lilly phrases this in a way that should become a mantra for all product managers: "Design like you're right; listen like you're wrong.[29]"

Building on the theme of trust, the best product managers are those who are guided by a strong and ethical point of view about the world. An ethics discussion can only get me into trouble, but it would be wrong not to at least touch on the subject. The point is that we're not just making products here. We are putting a stamp on the world, and we have the opportunity to make it a good one. To leave this place better than we found it. Perhaps

29. "Design like you're right..." – http://smashed.by/you-right

no one says it better than Mike Monteiro in *Design Is A Job*[30]:

> *I urge each and every one of you to seek out projects that leave the world a better place than you found it. We used to design ways to get to the moon; now we design ways to never have to get out of bed. You have the power to change that.*

How do we find projects and problems that fit these criteria? One way is to watch out for what Paul Graham calls schlep blindness[31], or our inability to identify hard problems to solve — mostly because we're just not consciously looking for them. Paul's advice to combat this? Instead of asking what problem you should solve, ask what problem you wish someone else would solve for you.

Another great source of worthy projects and ideas is the field of social entrepreneurship (pursuing innovative solutions to social problems). Meagan Fallone has a great overview of the nature and importance of this type of work[32]:

> *We in turn can teach Silicon Valley about the human link between the design function and the impact for a human being's quality of life. We do not regard the users of technology as "customers," but as human beings whose lives must be improved by the demystification of*

30. *Design Is A Job* – http://smashed.by/design-job
31. "Schlep Blindness" – http://www.paulgraham.com/schlep.html
32. "Technology Is Useless If It Doesn't Address A Human Need" – http://smashed.by/useless-tech

and access to technology. Otherwise, technology has no place in the basic human needs we see in the developing world. Sustainable design of technology must address real challenges; this is non-negotiable for us. Social enterprise stands alone in its responsibility to ensuring sustainability and impact in every possible aspect of our work.

The book Wicked Problems[33] is a great starting point for ideas on how to direct our efforts toward meaningful work.

Of course, we'll all have different definitions of work that's important and moves society forward. That's OK — what's important is to think it through, and have clear definitions and boundaries for the work you want to be involved in.

RESPONSIBLE AND FLEXIBLE

There is a well-known adage that product managers use to explain their role to others in an attempt to garner some sympathy. The saying goes that the most difficult part of being a product manager is that you have all the responsibility, but none of the authority. What we mean by this is that even though product managers are responsible for the success and failure of the product, they generally don't have anyone reporting to them. This is why communication and collaboration are such crucial characteristics for effective product managers.

---

33. *Wicked Problems: Problems Worth Solving* – https://www.wickedproblems.com/

The dangerous side of all having all the responsibility for a product is that it can lead to rigidity: an inability to let go of certain tasks that could easily be delegated, as well as a stubbornness to stick to an original plan even if circumstances have changed and a new course of action is needed. That's why PMs absolutely need to remain flexible. Planning is extremely important — we're going to spend a good third of this book talking about it. But an essential part of planning is to allow for the right information to change the plan if needed.

This flexibility can be disconcerting for PMs, but it's a necessary part of the process of building great products. So, get comfortable with ambiguity. There's a lot of it in this job.

In Fairness...

I'll end this section with a bonus characteristic. In fact, it's the most important characteristic of a product manager — the one that rules them all. I once had a discussion with a colleague in our development team about the new product development process we had rolled out a few months before. One of the words he used to describe the new process is *fair*.

It was a passing comment and I didn't really think much of it at the time, but since then I keep going back to that conversation, and the importance of fairness in the product management profession. All the characteristics I just talked about are great, but above all, fairness is the one that a PM simply cannot do without.

Let's look at one definition of the word fair[34], and what it means in the context of product management:

fair. *adjective*. free from favoritism or self-interest or bias or deception.

FREE FROM FAVORITISM

One of the fastest ways to become ineffective in a PM organization is to start playing favorites with a particular internal group, product line, or user base. As soon as people sense that you are not looking at all ideas and input equally and fairly, a lack of trust inevitably follows. And without trust, you'll have to work a lot harder (and longer) to bring people along for the ride on your roadmap.

FREE FROM SELF-INTEREST

If you start doing things purely with reasons like "because I want to" or "because I'm being measured by this metric," that same lack of trust grows very quickly. You cannot be effective by nursing your own pet projects and ignoring all the other needs around you.

FREE FROM BIAS

This often happens when PMs receive news they don't want to hear, especially from the user research or analytics teams. If something doesn't test well, don't make up

---

34. Definition of *fair* by the Free Online Dictionary, Thesaurus and Encyclopedia – http://www.thefreedictionary.com/fair

reasons why you are right and the users are wrong. Do the right thing and realign the design.

One of the hardest skills for a PM to learn is to take their own emotions and feelings out of the equation when it comes to decision-making. Yes, a lot of gut feeling goes into a product vision, but that cannot be based on personal preferences or preconceived ideas. This is much easier said than done, but something to strive for and be aware of at all times.

FREE FROM DECEPTION

This one seems obvious, but you see it often, especially when it comes to metrics and assessment. Don't ignore or distort negative data, or make a problem someone else's fault. The PM's job is to own a product — and this means owning its successes and its failures. You'll gain trust and respect if you not only claim the successes, but also acknowledge the failures and commit to do it better next time.

The PM role is often referred to as "the great diplomat," and with good reason. It is our responsibility to balance a variety of needs from inside and outside the business, and somehow turn that into a roadmap that delivers business value as well as meets user needs. A focus on fairness accomplishes that goal.

- **Fairness to users.** Approach users with respect, openness, and transparency. Understand their needs, and explain to them when you're doing something that makes it more difficult for them to meet those needs.

- **Fairness to the business.** Do everything you can to understand the needs of marketing, merchandising, customer support, and the rest. Pull them into the planning process, be clear about how projects are prioritized, and help them adjust to that process so they can define their project goals in the right way to get on the roadmap.

- **Fairness to technology.** Don't force the development team to make the technology do things it's not capable of doing. Understand the technical debt in the organization, and work actively to make those improvements part of regular development cycles.

A lot of this comes naturally in good product managers, but we need to be conscious of it every day. Fairness is a minimum required characteristic for an effective product manager. If you do it right, the real work of building great products can begin. But if you don't, you're dead in the water, working with a team that has no reason to trust that you're doing the right thing.

Where Product Management Fits Into An Organization

Here's some bad news. It doesn't matter how well PMs fit the ideal characteristics of the role, if they're sidelined in crucial discussions they just won't be effective. So another common question about product management is where it should fit into an organizational hierarchy. PMs are often described as mini-CEOs of their products, which should give a good indication of the appropriate hierarchical level PMs require to operate effectively.

Product management cannot sit within the marketing or engineering organizations — which unfortunately sometimes happens because companies aren't sure where to put it. To be effective, product management needs executive-level representation. In startups with one or two PMs, this means that they report directly to the CEO or COO. In larger organizations it means that the product management team is led by an executive-level person. In recent years, this has evolved into a new C-level role called the CPO (chief product officer).

The labels and job titles aren't as important as what this implies, though — which is that the product management team collaborates with fellow decision-makers in the company. Hiding PMs within an organization with very specific goals and agendas (like marketing or operations) defeats the purpose of developing and executing a holistic product vision and strategy.

I don't really like talking titles and hierarchy, so don't misunderstand this as a personal agenda to elevate PMs to godlike status. Instead, as you'll see throughout this book, PMs need to be at a decision-making level — whatever that is called in your company, and whether you have ten employees or ten thousand — in order to make the best possible products for the company and its users. That's all there is to it.

A Prerequisite For Success

There's one last topic we need to address before we get into the details of what PMs do day to day. An organization can hire the best product managers in the world, and implement the best development processes, but still fail if one non-negotiable prerequisite for success is not met. That prerequisite is this:

> *For product managers to succeed, there needs to be an executive mandate and company-wide understanding that even though everyone gets a voice, product decisions ultimately reside with product managers.*

This is a hard one to swallow for many companies — and another reason why I just argued that PMs need to have executive-level representation. When I mention this part in product management training courses, the mood in the room often changes. This is where people start complaining that even though they see the value in the product manager role, it will never work at their company, because leaders aren't willing to give up that ultimate control over the product. We'll discuss strategies to deal with this throughout the book, but for now here's a reminder of what Seth Godin reportedly once said: "Nothing is what happens when everyone has to agree." The product manager is there to make sure things happen — the *right* things.

Executive teams and individual contributors have to buy into this role. If they don't, product managers become impotent and frustrated bystanders to a process that continues to spiral out of control. And they'll end up going somewhere they're appreciated for the value they bring.

Coming Up Next...

In this chapter we covered a bunch of what might be considered soft issues in product management: what PMs are like, how they work with other people, what differentiates the good ones from the bad ones. It's tempting to skim over these issues to get to the how — the processes and day-to-day activities that make up the PM role. But that would be a mistake. I haven't seen a product development role that relies more on these kinds of soft skills for its success than that of the product manager. A PM can have the best strategy, and be brilliant at execution, but without the ability to work well with people and get them to rally around a common cause, they will fail. So if you've skipped over any of the sections in this chapter, now is a good time to go back and read them thoroughly!

Now that we have this foundation in place, it's time to move on to how product managers spend their days. We're going to break this into two sections: product planning (how to prepare for and prioritize product changes); and product execution (how to ship those changes). ❧

Part 2: Planning

CHAPTER 2:

Uncovering Needs

"If I had asked people what they wanted, they would have said faster horses." Far too often, we hear those words (supposedly spoken by Henry Ford) as a way to justify rushing headlong into executing a so-called innovation before the idea is tested with users. It's worth noting that not only did Henry Ford probably never speak those words, it also turns out that kind of thinking resulted in "a catastrophic loss of market share from which [Ford] never recovered[35]."

The lesson we should take from this story is that it's extremely dangerous to execute ideas without first identifying and testing assumptions about the value of those ideas. We shouldn't jump to a solution before we understand the problem. And that's what this section of the book is about.

I've already alluded to the two main elements of product management that we're going to discuss: product planning, and product execution. It's now time to expand on the product planning part. Below is a diagram of the framework we'll use to discuss the planning activities PMs are responsible for.

---

35. "Henry Ford, Innovation, and That 'Faster Horse' Quote", Patrick Vlaskovits, Harvard Business Review. – http://smashed.by/henry-ford

Product planning

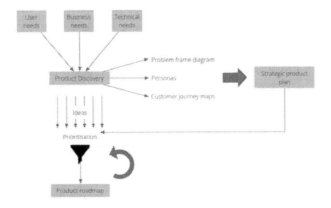

The primary steps of the product planning process, from identifying needs to developing a strategic and flexible roadmap

We'll start by looking at the different inputs into the product development process. The starting point is — always — needs. Not what we assume would be cool, but what users or the business need to be successful. Different inputs into this process include:

- **User needs.** The PM must have a good understanding of the market, the company's customers (existing and potential), and their behaviors and attitudes. PMs should never be caught off guard by questions about the product's target audience. We'll look at different sources of user input, including market research, user experience research, site analytics, and customer support.

- **Business needs.** The "putting users first" mantra too often neglects the fact that a product exists to make money.

Having revenue goals is not an excuse for bad design, though, so we'll look at the difference between bad revenue streams and good revenue streams.

- **Technical needs.** Development needs get ignored much of the time in favor of the more tangible front-end and business requirements. Developers know the limitations of the product; they know what needs to be fixed, and they know what technical debt needs to be paid. We'll discuss the mechanics of the all-important relationship between developers and PMs.

All these different needs feed into a process called product discovery. Once again, there are different definitions of this process, but I use the term here to refer to:

> *Defining the problem you are trying to solve for users, the business opportunities that exist to solve the problems, and the core competencies that will help you make the solution a success.*

The outputs of the product discovery process can vary — just like how long it takes can vary between anything from two to three hours to several weeks. In general, the product discovery process for larger projects produces outcomes like problem frame diagrams, personas, and customer journey maps — all of which we'll discuss in detail. These artifacts feed into the strategic product plan: a document that summarizes what the product is about, who it's for, and the plan to make it a success.

Once the strategy is set, the PM leads a process of idea generation (coming up with lots of different approaches to solve a problem) and iteration (quickly narrowing down those ideas to the best ones). This is followed by customer validation (testing ideas with target users) as part of a larger process to prioritize which ideas are worth pursuing. All these activities feed into the mighty product roadmap. There's quite a bit of controversy around the value and legitimacy of roadmaps, so we'll discuss that in detail (hint: it's not all bad).

Once the strategic product plan and the initial roadmap are in place, execution can start. Right now you're probably tempted to skip this section and jump straight to execution, but don't do it! One of the biggest dangers of product development is jumping to execution before an appropriate planning cycle has been completed, so we need to give planning the attention it deserves.

Let's start with gathering user needs.

User Needs

The first thing we need to clarify is the difference between *needs* and *features*. We often make the mistake of equating product features with user needs. If you've ever used a household appliance you'll know that this isn't the case. Have you ever used more than one or two of the preset cycles on your washing machine? And how many different ways do you need to toast your bread? The evolution of household appliances is a perfect example of what happens when features are equated with value. We don't need more ways to wash our clothes. We might need faster or quieter ways, sure. But as we know, more isn't necessarily better. And that's when users sometimes take matters into their own hands.

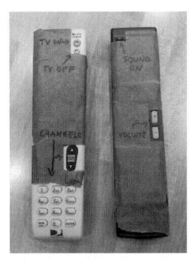

When the first reviews and usage statistics for Facebook Home[37] started appearing, John Gruber used a phrase that stuck with me[38]: "It's a well-designed implementation of an idea no one wants." Hyperbole aside, this is what happens when features (cover feed, friends filling the screen, chat heads, app launcher...) are mistaken for user needs (why would people want to replace their phone's operating system with an app?). The distinction

36. Reddit "My buddy dad-proofing his remotes" – http://smashed.by/remotes
37. "The Facebook Home disaster" – http://smashed.by/fb-home
38. "Facebook Home Is Looking Like a Flop" – http://smashed.by/fbflop

between features and needs is important, and sometimes difficult to spot. That's where user research comes in.

Research methods for gathering user needs are powerful because they rely more on observation and deduction than gathering answers to a bunch of predetermined questions. But before we get into the different methods we can use to make better products, we need to take a little detour to define some basic research terms.

First, we need to distinguish between quantitative research and qualitative research. With quantitative approaches, data tends to be collected indirectly from respondents, through methods like surveys and web analytics. Quantitative research allows you to understand what is happening, or how much of it is happening. With qualitative approaches, data is collected directly from participants in the form of interviews or usability tests. Qualitative research helps you understand how or why certain behaviors occur.

We also need to make a distinction between market research and user research. Both are important, but they serve different purposes. Market research seeks to understand the needs of a market in general. It is concerned with things like brand equity and market positioning. Attitudinal surveys and focus groups are the bread-and-butter tools for market researchers. They are tasked to figure out how to position a product in the market. Surveys and focus groups are very useful to understand market trends and needs, but they won't help you very much when it comes to the design of your product.

User research, on the other hand, focuses on users' interactions with a product. It is concerned with how people interact with technology, and what we can learn from their wants, needs, and frustrations. Those are the methods we'll focus on in this section.

So, with those definitions under our belts, let's look at some of the most common user research methods available to us. We can generally classify methods in three different buckets.[39]

1. EXPLORATORY RESEARCH

Exploratory research is most useful when the goal is to discover the most important (and often unmet) needs that users have with the products and services around them. This includes methods like contextual inquiries (also called ethnographic research or field visits), participatory design sessions, and concept testing. The goal here is to find out where there are gaps in the way existing products solve users' problems. New product or feature ideas often develop out of these sessions.

Make no mistake, this isn't about asking people if they want faster horses — it's about observing people and finding out that they want to get where they need to be much faster than they're currently able to. For example, we used to do a lot of ethnography with eBay sellers all over the world. By going into people's homes and seeing how they managed their sales, we uncovered a major issue that web analytics or surveys would never be able to tell us about. Sellers all manage their sales in different ways,

---

39. All of the methods I mention here — and more — are covered in detail in a book called *Observing The User Experience* by Elizabeth Goodman, Mike Kuniavsky, and Andrea Moed.

ranging from sticky notes stuck all around their monitors, to Excel spreadsheets with complicated formulas and pivot tables. Sellers were forced to make up their own process for something eBay should be helping them with: how to track sales progress, and learn from that. Through ethnography we uncovered an unmet user need that can be met with a variety of features on the site. But the need is the starting point.

2. DESIGN RESEARCH

Design research helps to develop and refine product ideas that come out of the user needs analysis. Methods include traditional usability testing, RITE testing (rapid iterative testing and evaluation), and even quantitative methods like eye tracking. This class of research helps us during the design process to create better products for the problems we're trying to solve for users. For example, we can build interactive prototypes and bring people into a usability lab, give them tasks to complete on the prototype, and uncover usability issues before we start the (expensive) development cycle. Since these are usually indepth one-to-one interviews, it's also a great opportunity to get more insight on how well certain features meet those customer needs we identified during exploratory research.

3. ASSESSMENT RESEARCH

Assessment research helps us figure out if the changes we've made really improve the product, or if we're just spinning our wheels for nothing. This class of research is often overlooked, but it's a crucial part of the product development cycle. Methods include surveys and web analytics to gives us a view of how our products perform over time, not just in terms of hard conversions, but also in terms of the attitudes of our users. These methods are most useful when combined with further design research to understand why we're seeing the changes we see. For example, form analytics can tell us where people abandon a form. Once we've made usability improvements to the form, it's important to assess if those changes made a difference to completion rates. Without assessment research we won't know if we're going in the right direction.

So, with this framework in mind, one of the first things a PM needs to do is find all the existing research that can help uncover user needs — both general (what the product needs to do to help users accomplish their goals) and specific (what's broken within or missing from the current solution). Grab any surveys, usability testing reports, and web analytics reports you can get your hands on, and drink it up. What users really want and need from a product must become part of the PM's fabric, and the only way to accomplish that is to get immersed in user data. Do whatever it takes: set up weekly customer calls, work the customer support queue a few hours a week, or set up regular usability testing sessions. User needs have to be a constant voice in the PM's ear when they start to balance all the other business and technology demands that are always pressing in — especially since those other demands are often in direct competition with user needs.

Business Needs

The web is littered with the remains of products that did a great job of fulfilling user needs, but never figured out a way to make money and become sustainable businesses. Over the past few years we've seen several beloved services on the web shut down because of a lack of revenue. Editorially was a fantastic collaborative writing and editing tool whose creators eventually realized that "Even if all of our users paid up, it wouldn't be enough.[40]"

A few months before that, the photo startup Everpix shut its doors, in part because it couldn't afford the cloud storage bills. This happened despite having thousands of paying users on the platform. The founders later admitted that even though they were able to make a product that people genuinely loved, they spent too much time working on that product, and not enough time on growth and distribution.[41]

These stories are complex and there are never easy answers. Yet it's a common approach on the web to focus on getting as many users as possible as quickly as possible, and then figuring out how to make money out of them later. Call me old school if you must, but that's just no way to build a business. I'm not saying a new product needs to be profitable from day one (although that would be nice, of course), but there at least needs to be a plan — a

---

40. "Goodbye" – http://smashed.by/editorially-goodbye
41. "Out of the picture: why the world's best photo startup is going out of business"
    – http://smashed.by/photo-startup

few possible revenue streams — that will eventually lead to a sustainable business[42].

So where do these revenue stream ideas come from? Well, in many cases they come from customers; the research methods discussed above can also be used to figure out what people would be willing to pay for — and how much. But there are also several internal teams that spend most of their time thinking about business needs, and the PM needs to form strong allies with these teams. This includes the business development team, the sales and marketing teams, and the engineering team (yes, the engineering team — no one knows the product better than they do).

When it comes to growing the business, it's useful to split activities into two buckets: eliminating bad revenue streams, and pursuing good revenue streams.

ELIMINATING BAD REVENUE STREAMS

The Greek tragedian Sophocles once wrote, "Profit is sweet, even if it comes from deception." We have to be wary of our own frailties when it comes to making money. Deceiving people to make a quick buck might seem like a good idea at the time, but it is a short-term strategy that is bound to backfire — not to mention that it doesn't exactly fit with the ethical characteristic we discussed earlier.

In interface design we refer to deceptive techniques as dark patterns. A dark pattern is a type of interface that is

---

42. Unless you're only in it for the acqui-hire, but that's a different story altogether.

specifically designed to trick people into buying stuff they don't want. There are many examples, and the website http://www.darkpatterns.org/ provides a comprehensive list, but these techniques include examples like these:

- Ryanair buries the option to opt out of travel insurance in an unrelated dropdown menu so most people don't realize they're buying the insurance.

- Some iOS apps for kids, like Talking Tom Cat, put random pop-ups on the screen at all points in the game to trick kids into making in-app purchases.

- On login, PayPal often shows a full-screen ad with only a small link at the top-right to close the ad and continue to your account section.

- Zynga's game FarmVille was "engineered with one goal in mind: to coerce users into tending their virtual plots of land for as long as possible[43]."

It might seem obvious to point out that some revenue streams are not ethical, and therefore not worth pursuing. The problem is that, very often, these methods work — they unfortunately do make money (at least in the short term). But they also have long-term consequences that are rarely considered. Once users figure out what's going on and start complaining, these underhanded methods affect companies directly in the form of increased support costs and major reputation damage.

43. "The Zynga Abyss" – http://smashed.by/zynga-abyss

Ryanair has become a poster child for dark patterns because of its insurance tactics. That's not a good position to be in.

The thing is, very few people start their days thinking, "I wonder how I could deceive people today?" Instead, dark patterns and deceptive methods sneak up on most product managers as potentially decent ideas that degenerate little by little until they become dark patterns. We shouldn't spend much time on this, except to say: watch out. Don't fall into the dark pattern trap. An easy, obvious, but rarely applied rule of thumb is to ask of any potential revenue opportunity: "Would I be OK with it if a product asked me to do or pay for this?" If the answer is no, walk away. There are better paths out there. It might be more difficult to find those paths, but it's worth sacrificing short-term success for long-term loyalty from customers. And besides, you'll sleep better at night.

Sometimes a revenue stream starts out as a good idea, but a change in the external environment turns it into something undesirable. The problem is that by then it might already be a large source of revenue, which places the business in quite a predicament.

One such example is photos in search results on eBay. Back in 1995 when eBay was founded, storage was expensive. So it made sense to charge users a nominal amount to upload a photo to their listings. Fast forward a decade to 2005, and not only was storage cheap, but the idea of charging users to add photos to their listings seemed ludicrous. The problem was that by then, charging for photos was a significant revenue stream, so it was not an easy decision to make photos free.

Our user experience team partnered with the analytics team to reveal that showing photos in search results by default not only increased sales, but also had a positive impact on ratings of search results organization and helpfulness. It took a while, but eventually eBay made the brave decision to shut off that bad revenue stream and make photos free (for up to eight photos), and it never looked back.

When it comes to dealing with these accidental bad revenue streams, the best course of action is to conduct research to understand needs and motivations, coupled with A/B testing to get an accurate measure of the effect it would have on good revenue when the bad revenue stream is cut off.

PURSUING GOOD REVENUE STREAMS

Good revenue streams can come from many different sources. Consumers are willing to pay for things as long as the value is immediately clear to them. And the entire product management process is built around finding that value first, and then building a product and business around it, as opposed to making something and then scrambling to find the value. So, user needs research is always the first place to look for how the product can make money.

Consider the slightly offbeat example of Iron Maiden (yes, really). The band has spent a significant amount of time touring in South America, and it's turned out to be a great strategy. They usually play sold out, highly profitable shows in the region. Why has the band been so successful there? If you ask music analytics company Music-metric, they'll tell you it's related to an unlikely phenomenon: piracy. The company discovered a surge of BitTorrent traffic related to Iron Maiden's music in South America in recent years, particularly in Brazil. By going where people were already fans of the music the band was able, as Musicmetric CEO Gregory Mead put it, to "[be] rather successful in turning free file-sharing into fee-paying fans[44]." Understanding where your users are already highly invested in your product is the best way to figure out what value they would be willing to pay for.

Once there are existing revenue streams, there are several standard growth strategies, such as expanding to new regions, establishing new channels, appealing to a broader market, and building new products for an existing market. But there is one strategy in particular that I'd like to focus on, because it's a comprehensive approach to long-term business success. It's a strategy formalized by Brandon Schauer at Adaptive Path, and it's called the long wow[45]. To quote from Brandon's article about it:

> The Long Wow is a means to achieving long-term customer loyalty through systematically impressing your customers again and again. Going a step beyond just measuring loyalty, the Long Wow is an experience-centric approach to fostering and creating it.

The long wow is built on a four-step process:

---

44. "How Iron Maiden turned piracy into paying customers" – http://smashed.by/piracy

45. "The Long Wow" – http://smashed.by/long-wow

1. **Know your platform for delivery.** Identify the ways you can combine different ways to engage with customers, both online and offline.

2. **Tackle a wide area of unmet customer needs.** Based on your user needs research, identify an area where there is a huge need that is not met by your product, or any other products out there.

3. **Create and evolve your repeatable process.** Combine the company's existing strengths with new ideas to meet unmet needs to come up with ways to delight users over and over.

4. **Plan and stage wow experiences.** Develop your ideas over time, and introduce new and better experiences consistently along the product development life cycle.

And then, repeat as necessary to make sure the long wow isn't just a one-time thing. This is an excellent way to identify good revenue streams in your product, and ensure that you continue to provide the value needed to create loyal customers who keep giving you money.

Technical Needs

The first thing we need to be clear about when it comes to technical needs is that, just as in finance, there is a huge difference between assets and debt. Technical assets are things like the underlying technologies your product is built on, backoffice systems (procurement, finance, fulfillment), and scaling technologies (sysadmin activities).

In contrast, technical debt refers to systems and code that place strain on your product (in the form of bugs and scaling issues) and gets worse the longer it isn't addressed. According to Steve McConnell[46] there are two kinds of technical debt:

- **Unintentional debt** occurs when the wrong technical design is implemented, or a programmer just writes bad code. This kind of debt is non-strategic, and you want as little of it as possible.

- **Intentional debt** occurs when the organization knows that what they're doing isn't ideal, but it's a compromise worth making for whatever reason (usually to do with budget or time constraints). Although not ideal, this kind of debt is inevitable in any organization. It needs to be minimized and dealt with, but unlike unintentional debt, it is not entirely unavoidable.

There are many obvious reasons to avoid, minimize, and pay down technical debt. But the most salient argument is to avoid what's commonly referred to as the broken windows theory[47]. This criminological theory aims to explain the effect of urban disorder and vandalism and states that:

> [M]aintaining and monitoring urban environments in a well-ordered condition may stop further vandalism and escalation into more serious crime.

46. "Technical Debt" – http://smashed.by/technical-debt
47. Broken windows theory – http://smashed.by/broken-windows

The basic analogy is that software is like an urban environment. As soon as a few broken windows (bad code) appear in the environment, and those windows are not immediately repaired, the tendency is for vandals to break a few more windows (we stop caring about good code). Then the environment starts to deteriorate: litter appears, squatters show up, and so on (all coding standards go out the window). Before long, all hell breaks loose. To quote Steve McConnell[48] again:

> *If the debt grows large enough, eventually the company will spend more on servicing its debt than it invests in increasing the value of its other assets. A common example is a legacy code base in which so much work goes into keeping a production system running (i.e., 'servicing the debt') that there is little time left over to add new capabilities to the system.*

That's a situation that that needs to be avoided at all costs, and it's where the product manager comes in. Finding space on the roadmap to address technical debt is usually an extremely tough sell. Paying down debt is not sexy — you usually can't see any changes in the front end, very few people understand what's going on so there is a fair bit of skepticism about why the work is needed, and no one really wants to go clean up litter in the code. But it's essential to prioritize technical debt in most, if not every, development cycle, to avoid the breakdown of basic services until there is nothing left but a ghost town.

---

48. "Technical Debt" – http://smashed.by/technical-debt

It's important to note that technical debt isn't necessarily bad at the moment it occurs. Sometimes technical
debt allows a feature-rich release to happen when it otherwise wouldn't have if there was a zero-tolerance approach to technical debt. In general, new debt is OK, old
debt is bad. Henrik Kniberg proposes a great way to deal
with out of control technical debt in his article "Good and
Bad Technical Debt[49]". He introduces the concept of a
debt ceiling, where you stop to make sure the debt doesn't
get out of control:

> *When debt hits the ceiling, we declare "debt alert!", the
> doors are closed, all new development stops, and every-
> body focuses on cleaning up the code until they're all the
> way back down to the baseline.*

Ideally you'll address technical debt during every development cycle, but sometimes you're going to hit that ceiling, and then it's important to stop and work on it before
it's too late.

Putting It All Together

Gathering user needs, business needs, and technical
needs is one thing. Figuring out where to put all this information and what to do with it is something else entirely. You need a system to gather and structure all this input in a way that will not only make sense later, but make

---

49. "Good and Bad Technical Debt (and how TDD helps)" – http://smashed.by/
good-bad-debt

it easy to repurpose the information in different formats, as needed.

Everyone has their own preferences and systems for keeping notes and organizing information, but there are a few ways this process can be made easier. First off, don't use standalone tools — like email or Microsoft Word — that don't integrate well with others. This kind of siloed content is difficult to share, difficult to keep up to date, and difficult to format for other purposes.

My preferred way of gathering and sorting information is the simplest file format we have at our disposal: plain text files, preferably tagged using a controlled vocabulary. I love that with plain text the focus is on the words, not the formatting. I love that it's portable and can be used anywhere and everywhere, in any piece of software that edits or displays words. I love how easy it is to create beautifully formatted documents when needed. Most of all, I love how fast it is. I simply work more efficiently since switching to plain text.

For example, as a Mac user, I take all my notes using Brett Terpstra's nvALT[50]. The two main things I love about nvALT are:

- Modeless operation in which searching for notes and creating new notes happen in the same part of the interface. It's highly efficient and there's zero lag.

- Powerful keyboard shortcuts for mouseless operation, which further speeds up your writing.

---

50. nvALT – http://smashed.by/nvalt

These files all sync to a folder on Dropbox, which makes the notes immediately accessible on all my other devices (I use Notesy[51] for note-taking on my iOS devices). But what about formatting? That's where Markdown[52] comes in. Markdown is an easy-to-learn, inconspicuous syntax that lets you focus on what you're writing without getting bogged down in what it's going to look like once you're done. At the same time, it's a powerful system for formatting documents automatically when you need to print them out, or send something to a colleague or client. The syntax remains easily readable without getting in the way of your words.

When these notes have to be shared in more formal documents, it's still important to stay away from offline tools like Microsoft Word. Company wikis, or tools like Google Docs are great for collaboration and to share information about the various needs and research you collect over time.

So, assuming you now have a way to collect, store, and share all this information, the next question is what to do with it. We'll get into prioritization in an upcoming chapter, but for now, suffice to say that it's important to strike a balance between addressing user, business, and technical needs, and that how this balance changes is based on three main factors:

- **The stage of the product in its life cycle.** Is it a brand new product, or has it been around for a while?

---

51. Notesy – http://smashed.by/notesy
52. Markdown – http://smashed.by/markdown

- **The level of user engagement.** Are you struggling to gain traction, or are users beating down the door to use your product?

- **The financial state of the business.** Are you still figuring out how to make money, or is there a steady revenue stream?

Depending on how those three factors are put together, you will have a different focus on your product development. Is the product brand new, and in a heavy acquisition phase? Then user needs should carry more weight. Is the business seeing massive organic growth? Then put more focus on scaling and revenue growth.

Acquisition phase

Growth phase

Balancing user, business, and technical needs based on the phase of the business

This approach will give the PM a rough idea of how priorities and needs should be balanced, but it's a long way from figuring out what to build, and how and when to do it.

The point that deserves to be stressed is this: without doing the work to understand the core user, business, and technical needs that your product will address, you'll be building a foundation on sand. The product might work for a while, but eventually something better will come along. So instead of relying on dangerous assumptions, build a sustainable product on the solid rock of real insights.

Of course, uncovering needs is one thing. Figuring out how to turn those insights into a successful product is something else entirely. So let's discuss why so many products fail, and what we can do to make sure ours don't go down that road. ❧

CHAPTER 3:

Product Discovery

Brasília is a remarkable, bizarre city. The vision of architect Oscar Niemeyer[53], it was built in just four years, from 1956 to 1960. More than fifty years later, its beauty and elegance are renowned. But Brazil's capital city is known for something else as well: how difficult it is to live there. A "shiny citadel" from far away, as the Guardian once reported[54], up close Brasília has "degraded into a violent, crime-ridden sprawl of cacophonous traffic jams. The real Brazil has spilled into its utopian vision."

This problem echoes across today's web landscape as well, where the needs of ordinary users spill constantly into companies' utopian visions. All around us we see beautiful, empty monuments erected not for their users, but for the people who built them — and the VCs who are scouting them. Even sites and apps that go beyond beauty to usability often fail because they can't find a big enough market.

Why can't some interactive products find enough users to be sustainable? Why are there so many failed startups, despite a renewed focus on design? Most importantly, what can we do about it?

---

53. http://smashed.by/niemeyer
54. "Trouble in utopia as the real Brazil spills into Niemeyer's masterpiece" – http://smashed.by/brazil

The Rise Of Usable, Useless Products

We've long accepted that for a product to be useful, it needs to have acceptable levels of both utility ("whether it provides the features you need") and usability ("how easy & pleasant these features are to use[55]"). Yet far too often, we seem to ignore the former in favor of the latter, ending up with lots of easy and pleasant applications that have no reason to exist. One could argue that the first version of the iOS app Color fell into this trap[56].

One of the major problems that new products in particular run into is a lack of product/market fit[57], as we've discussed in chapter 1 where we defined the roles and responsibilities of the product manager:

> *Product/market fit means being in a good market with a product that can satisfy that market.*

The problem arises when startups and companies don't spend enough time increasing the likelihood of good product/market fit before they start design and development. The lean startup concept of minimum viable product[58] (just those features that allow the product to be deployed, and no more) is certainly useful, but we might rather want to focus on minimum desirable products[59]:

---

55. "Usability 101: Introduction to Usability" – http://smashed.by/usability-101
56. See "How Color Already Blew It" – http://smashed.by/color
57. "Product/Market Fit" – http://smashed.by/market-fit
58. See the Wikipedia article: http://smashed.by/minimum-viable-product
59. See Andrew Chen's article "Minimum Desirable Product" – http://smashed.by/mdp

Minimum Desirable Product is the simplest experience
necessary to prove out a high-value, satisfying product
experience for users.

What's the use of fast iteration if all it does is get us to a
suboptimal solution more quickly, when there might be a
much better solution out there?

But before we get ahead of ourselves and discuss how
to fix this, let's jump into some of the all-important why
questions.

Why Products Fail To Fit

Brasília's biggest problem is that the architects who designed it didn't consider how the city could be used if mil-
lions of people lived there. They exhibited architectural
myopia[60] by focusing so intently on the design task that
they weren't able to adequately consider the needs of people. I've written before about a similar phenomenon in
our industry: designer myopia[61]. Lured by the recognition
(and clients and VCs) they desire, designers are often primarily focused on being featured in galleries and list-dri-
ven blog posts that drive tons of traffic.

There is nothing inherently wrong with that need for
recognition — but it becomes a problem when it hurts
users. If Brasília teaches us anything, it's that becoming
blind to the needs of users leads us down a dangerous

---

60. See "Shareable: Architectural Myopia: Designing for Industry, Not People" –
    http://smashed.by/architectural-myopia
61. "Designer Myopia: How To Stop Designing For Ourselves" –
    http://smashed.by/designer-myopia

path where we lose control over our products, with no way to get it back. Once something has shipped, you can either iterate or pivot. Iteration is great if you're on the right path. Pivoting is dangerous because changing course can wreak havoc on employees and users alike.

Product Discovery: A Better Way

If we want to create better, more useful products, we need to stop designing solutions too early and start instead with product discovery: a process that helps us understand the problem properly so we don't just design things better, but design better things.

Product discovery consists of three steps:

1. Frame the problem.

2. Explore and assess multiple solutions.

3. Prioritize and plan.

Let's discuss each of these steps in detail.

1. FRAME THE PROBLEM

It's hard to argue with these words, attributed to Einstein:

> *If I had an hour to solve a problem I'd spend 55 minutes thinking about the problem and 5 minutes thinking about solutions.*

Step one of product discovery is that proverbial fifty-five minutes. Here, the product manager leads a process to answer questions such as:

- Which user needs and problems are we trying to solve? For existing products, what are the shortcomings we need to fix?

- What are the profiles of our users (personas)?

- What customer insights are available to inform the solution (customer support, analytics, market research, user research, competitive analysis, and so on)?

- How will solving this problem help our business?

- What makes our business capable of solving this problem?

- How will we measure success?

This is where the PM pulls out all their notes on user needs, business needs, and technical needs to seed and guide a discussion about the essence of the product. There are several techniques to structure the discussion and make it easier to get to the bottom of these questions. Fishbone diagrams and the five whys are two root-cause analysis techniques that can be applied very effectively to defining a problem in terms of user needs and business goals.

Fishbone Diagrams

These are mostly used as a quality control method in manufacturing, but the technique has since found its way into the world of digital product design. The diagram is created by identifying a problem or a desired outcome, and then listing all aspects that could be a cause of the problem or outcome. When used in the context of product development, these causes are usually grouped in categories commonly referred to as the seven Ps: product (service), price, place, promotion, people, process, and physical evidence.

The Five Whys

This is a similar technique that uses iterative questioning to find the root cause of a problem. The basic idea is to state a problem and keep asking why — sometimes more than five times — until a particular process can be identified that is the main cause of the problem.

This phase always — without fail — produces insights the team finds incredibly valuable. Startups gain clarity about what to say yes and no to in their product, and large corporations learn how to go beyond customer-centric buzzwords and discover which benefits they should be selling to their users. As just one of many examples, I was once in a workshop that revealed the executives had a completely different vision for the company than the designers and developers. It was an awkward two hours, but in the end they agreed on the tough but correct decision to suspend their e-commerce plans until some of the content areas on the site had been sorted out. It's great to see a statement of purpose emerge from these sessions — one that finally gets an organization to agree on what the product's focus should be.

From this step, the PM produces a problem frame diagram, which is simply a visual summary of the main takeaways in the form of three overlapping circles: user needs, business goals, and core competencies.

Example of a problem frame diagram (Larger view[62])

Every decision the team makes should be anchored in at least one of these circles — preferably in the overlap of all

---

62. http://smashed.by/problem-frame-diagram

three. Design decisions should focus on meeting those needs and capitalizing on the business opportunities by using the core competencies identified.

This is also a good point in the process to create personas for your target market. There are great resources available for the creation of personas[63], so I won't go into it into much detail beyond a quick summary.

Personas are hypothetical, archetypal user characters, defined in detail. They have names and faces, so the whole team can picture them. As opposed to a mythical average user, they are solid people we can imagine using our product to achieve their goals. This is helpful because by focusing on individuals that are closer to the edges of the experience, instead of the average, we're able to cater to a larger portion of the user base.

In the documentary Objectified[64], Dan Formosa from Smart Design says, "What we need to do to design is to look at the extremes. The middle will take care of itself." As an example, he talks about how they once designed garden shears specifically to cater for people with arthritis. They knew that if the shears worked for that user, it would work well for everyone. That's the power of personas.

So we develop personas for a few important reasons:

- **To capture knowledge.** The team identifies what characteristics of users matter most for the product's design

---

63. *The Persona Lifecycle: Keeping People in Mind Throughout Product Design* by John Pruitt, Tamara Adlin; and *The User is Always Right: A Practical Guide to Creating and Using Personas for the Web* by Steve Mulder, Ziv Yaar.
64. http://www.objectifiedfilm.com/

(such as technological savviness, family size, and so on), and then use those characteristics to pick users that make up the target market.

- **To build consensus.** Personas are a good starting point for team members to clarify who they think users are. Even if everyone disagrees at first, it's a great process to reach agreement on whom to target.

- **To build empathy.** We constantly need to be reminded that we are not our users, so our needs are a distant second to their needs. Personas help us to put ourselves into the mindsets of the people who will use our products. It's useful to get very specific and create different scenarios of how personas might use the product in a certain situation.

- **To guide a design that maximizes usability.** Personas help to settle design arguments. Teams can be confident that if a product can fulfill each persona's needs, they have achieved their goals.

It's worth pointing out that not everyone is a fan of personas. Personas can become oversimplified caricatures of users that don't take specific situations and actions into account. Without proper research, personas also tend to be shallow and not very useful. But those dangers are easy to avoid. Remember that personas aren't prescriptive, they're *descriptive*. You can't identify a persona and then try to predict people's behavior from it. But with solid research and analysis you can use personas effectively to help focus development efforts on target users, and help define what features should be included in (and just as importantly, excluded from) the product.

Practical traveller

Willem (52)

Accountant
Durbanville

Willem lives in Durbanville, and he is an accountant at a mid-sized paper merchant. He likes his job, but he lives for the weekends, when he can spend time with his wife and 2 kids, and his braai.

Willem loves watching sport on TV, and he still reads Die Burger faithfully every morning. He drives a Toyota Corolla, but his prize possession is a BMW motorcycle that he takes out for a spin on weekends.

Willem flies to JHB for work once a month, and his PA rents a car for him for a day or two to get around.

Each July he flies his family up to Durban for the school holidays. They stay with his wife's grandparents, and they always rent a car so they can explore the area together as a family.

Willem always chooses the cheapest, safest car for his family on these trips. He makes sure there's aircon in the car, but only gets basic insurance cover.

I mostly travel for business, so I care about safety and affordability

GOALS

- To get around while he's on business.
- To keep his family comfortable and safe during holidays.

TRAVEL DRIVERS

- Risk
- Price sensitive
- Packaged
- Shared
- Flexible
- Roughing it

Example of a persona (Larger view[65])

Customer journey maps are another useful output of the product discovery process. Journey maps are visual representations that help summarize research, highlight and

---

65. http://smashed.by/persona-example

prioritize user needs and opportunities, and get buy-in from stakeholders. A product's journey map is important because:

- It confirms a common understand of the users' needs and goals, and the strategy you intend to follow to attend to those needs and goals.

- It is an excellent prioritization tool, since it allows companies to focus on the most important parts of an experience first, without losing sight of the overall picture.

- It is a guiding light for design. Every time a design idea comes along, a quick glance at the journey map helps us figure out if it's a good idea that will accomplish the chosen strategy.

- It is an excellent conduit for content-first design, which fits in perfectly with responsive design approaches.

There are many different ways to create a customer journey map. It has some common elements, such as a visual representation of customer touchpoints, emotions, and key takeaways throughout their experience with a product. But that's only useful up to a point, so we've started to expand on the concept. In addition to the usual elements, this document also becomes a representation of the information architecture and the product's content plan, with personas (needs, goals, scenarios) serving as the starting point for everything — the glue that ties it all together.

This document is a summary of everything we need to know to design the best possible product for users. It has the following elements:

- **Unique selling points** to keep us focused on what the site needs to communicate at all times. This comes straight from the persona needs and goals.

- **Journey stages and model** to remind us how the product fits into people's lives, and what the primary calls to action need to be throughout the site. This section is a visual representation of a customer's journey, from realizing they might have a need for the product until long after they've used it. This helps PMs keep a holistic view of the entire product and how it fits into users' daily lives.

- **Questions** that our target personas are likely to ask in each phase of the journey, to focus the type of content we serve on each page. In an e-commerce context, these are questions like, "Can I trust this retailer?" or "When will my stuff arrive?"

- **Takeaways and key principles** to summarize the unique selling points, journey model, and user questions, and document how they translate into the design decisions and solutions we need to keep in mind throughout the design process.

- **Content plan** that maps each phase of the journey with the questions our personas will ask during that phase, and what it means for the specific content that needs to go on each page. We get very specific here — nothing gets on the page unless it's in the content plan. And if we can't identify a persona that would find the content useful, it doesn't go on the list.

Example customer journey map (Larger view[66])

Journey maps are often the culmination of weeks or months of product discovery work. It might seem like a large investment, but you'll be thankful you made it once the execution phases start. It's a document that, above all, keeps teams sane because it focuses their attention on what's important.

Once the problem has been defined (and agreed on by all stakeholders), it's time to start thinking about solutions.

---

66. http://smashed.by/customer-journey-map

2. EXPLORE AND ASSESS MULTIPLE SOLUTIONS

The takeaways from problem-framing lead into a period of divergent thinking, where you produce as many different possible solutions as quickly as possible — visually. Break out the pencils, and lots and lots of paper.

Rather than open your laptop too early in the design process, you can use sketching to produce a variety of solutions in a short amount of time. It's important to generate as many different ideas as possible during this stage of the process. To understand why this is important, let's go to mathematical theory, specifically the concepts of maxima and minima[67]:

> In mathematics, the maximum and minimum [...] of a function [...] are the largest and smallest value that the function takes at a point either within a given neighborhood (local or relative extremum) or on the function domain in its entirety (global or absolute extremum).

Using the concept of local neighborhoods and global functions as backdrop, let's look at the idea of the local maximum within the context of product development. For the purposes of product development, I liken the mathematical concept of neighborhood to product. For example, the iPhone (as a product) will hit a local maximum when the current design cannot be improved any more given the time constraints and market conditions. This isn't necessarily the best product you can make in

---

67. Maxima and minima – http://smashed.by/max-min

the entire industry (global maximum), but it is the best iteration of the current product.

To understand this fully we also have to differentiate between the concepts of iteration and variation. Variation is a way to explore a bunch of alternative product solutions. In contrast, iteration solidifies the product idea that gets chosen. To quote Jon Kolko[68]: "Where an iteration moves an idea forward (or backwards), a variation moves an idea left or right." Or, to put it into the language of maxima and minima, variation surveys the global landscape to help companies choose the right neighborhood (product) to move into. Iteration then helps them to find the local maximum in their chosen neighborhood.

This is why generating lots of ideas quickly through sketching is so important. The variation ensures that teams spend enough time finding the right neighborhood for their product before they buy the land, so to speak, and start developing their product. In an answer to the question "Should I focus on a good user experience, or push something out quickly?" Ryan Singer wrote a good answer on Quora[69] that provides a summary of why product solution variation is so important:

Design is a path-dependent process. That means the early moves constrain the later moves. On the very first iteration the design possibilities are wide open. The designer defines some screens and workflows and then the pro-

---

68. "Iteration and Variation" – http://smashed.by/iteration-variation
69. Ryan Singer's answer to "Should I focus on a good user experience, or push something out quickly?" – http://smashed.by/ryan-singer

grammer builds those. On the next iteration, it's not wide open anymore. The new design has to fit into the existing design, and the new code needs to fit into the existing code. Old code can be changed, but you don't want to scrap everything. There is a pressure to keep moving with what is already there.

Our early design decisions are like bets whose outcome we will have to live with iteration after iteration. Since that's the case, there is a strong incentive to be sure about our early bets. In other words, we want to reduce uncertainty on the first iterations.

Now, much has been said about the value of sketching, but I'd like to add a couple more thoughts about it here. Even though I don't like the word very much, I do like the concept of "thinkering", a word that Michael Ondaatje coined in his novel *The English Patient* to describe the creation of ideas in the mind while tinkering with the hands. Michele and Robert Root-Bernstein describe it as follows[70]:

> *[t]he physical manipulation of things, like direct personal experience of any kind, generates sensory images of all sorts and thus enables thought. Hands-on tinkering leads to minds-on thinkering. Bodily engagement with nature teaches much more than any amount of words or numbers in science books. Doing produces a personal understanding that symbols simply can't.*

70. "Thinkering" – http://smashed.by/thinkering

And that's why sketching is much better for the initial idea variation phase of a project than jumping straight into design software. And by the way — everyone can sketch. If you don't believe me, Dan Roam's book *The Back of the Napkin*[71] will convince you otherwise. It's a great resource for helping you figure out how to solve problems with sketching.

The outcomes of this phase of the process are storyboards and low-fidelity sketches to help visualize possible solutions to the problems you've identified. The goal is to get these ideas in front of potential users as quickly as possible to get their feedback and validate your assumptions. However, first you need to narrow the ideas down to a manageable set, otherwise you'll be testing hypotheses forever and never ship anything.

3. PRIORITIZE AND PLAN

I talk to many teams who complain about analysis paralysis: an inability to make decisions because there are just too many factors (and people) involved. Good prioritization methods give teams reassurance that even though they're not focusing on everything at once, they are focused on the right information to make good decisions.

You can do this with a phase of convergent thinking that narrows down which ideas and solutions to explore further. There are many established processes for this

---

71. *The Back of the Napkin: Solving Problems and Selling Ideas with Pictures* by Dan Roam
    – http://smashed.by/napkin

type of prioritization, each designed for a different scenario. Let's take a look at three of these methods.

KJ-Method

With the KJ-Method (also called affinity diagrams), you group similar issues together and use a voting mechanism to rank those issues in order of importance. It's best when you have a large group of stakeholders who all have strong opinions about the product and you want to make decisions quickly. The basic outline of a KJ session is as follows:

- Write each idea or need on a sticky note.

- Put all the sticky notes on the wall, adding more if additional ideas are sparked in the process.

- Group similar ideas or needs together.

- Assign a name to each group, staying away from jargon (try to use plain, user-focused language).

- Rank the ideas or needs in order of importance by voting on them. Each person in the group gets a set number of votes (usually three) to give to the ideas or needs they feel are most important (use markers or small stickers as the mechanism to cast votes). They can distribute the votes however they want — all three on a single idea they think is extremely important, or distributed across three different ideas.

The KJ-Method is remarkably effective to reach agreement on the priority of issues that need to be addressed, even in large teams. It's a great method to give everyone a voice and a chance to make the case for why they believe a specific idea or need is important to the business.

Kano Model

Developed in the 1980s by Professor Noriaki Kano for the Japanese automotive industry, the Kano model is a helpful method to prioritize product features by plotting them on the following two-dimensional scale:

- How well a particular user need is being fulfilled by a feature.

- What level of satisfaction the feature will give users.

The model is generally used to classify features into three groups:

- **Excitement generators:** delightful, unexpected features that make a product both useful and usable.

- **Performance payoffs:** features that continue to increase satisfaction as improvements are made.

- **Basic expectations:** features that users expect as a given — if these aren't available in a product, you're in trouble.

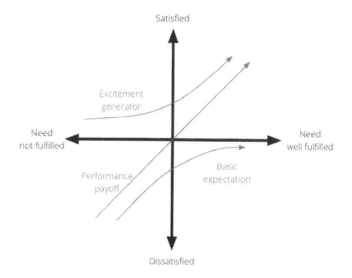

Satisfied

Excitement
generator

Need
not fulfilled

Need
well fulfilled

Performance
payoff

Basic
expectation

Dissatisfied

Using the Kano model to balance feature development

This method works when you want to ensure you have a balanced roadmap that addresses basic requirements, as well as innovative features that might help the product pull ahead of competitors.

Amazon.com's Approach

Amazon's approach prioritizes large themes first, before going into individual features and projects to address those themes. Ian McAllister describes the starting phase of this approach[72] as follows:

---

72. Ian McAllister's answer to "Product Management: What are the best ways to prioritize a list of product features?" – http://smashed.by/mcallister

Prioritize themes, not projects. Create a list of themes for your product or business. Examples might be customer acquisition, activation, retention, avg revenue per user, avg visits per user, etc. Pick ~3 that are the most important for your product given its stage.

The next steps involve assigning people to work on each of the themes, generating projects within each of the themes, and then prioritizing each project based on the potential cost and business impact of each. It's a good approach when the sheer number of features or improvements required feels overwhelming, and you need a way to structure and make sense of all of them.

I've personally found a stripped-down version of the Amazon method most effective and realistic in organizations I've worked with. As much as I agree with the principles of each of the three approaches mentioned above, they tend to become unrealistic in the context of ongoing prioritization. So here is the extremely simple process we've used, with good results:

- Have a whiteboard with a permanent two-by-two matrix on it. The horizontal axis represents business impact (which includes user needs and technical considerations), and the vertical axis represents the level of effort to implement (which includes people and their time commitment).

- Write product requests and ideas on sticky notes as they come up, have a quick discussion with relevant people to ascertain business value and level of effort, and then put the sticky note on the two-by-two matrix.

- Write prioritization numbers next to each of the features or themes, starting with those that have the highest business value. I like a 70/30 split between high- and low-effort features.

- Every week or so, check your roadmap to make sure you're still working on the right things, and make adjustments as needed.

Prioritizing using business impact and level of effort indicators

It's a simple method, and it's far from perfect. But it has a few things going for it:

- It's detailed enough to ensure constant prioritization based on what's important.

- It's light enough to make it practical for everyday use.

These methods all work because they facilitate teamwork without falling into the traps of design by committee. Everyone gets a voice, but not everyone gets to make decisions. That's an essential attribute of any good prioritization method, because as Seth Godin says, "Nothing is what happens when everyone has to agree."

In addition to providing the necessary structure to reach prioritization decisions quickly, these methods also produce tangible artifacts that can help you sell your ideas to internal stakeholders. User experience is often much less a design problem than it is an organizational problem. As much as we just want to do our work without obstruction, we can only be truly effective if we also make a compelling argument to people in other parts of the organization. These structured prioritization methods make that step reasonably painless by helping you produce written and visual records of your thought process.

But what's more important than the specific method being used, is that you come out of the prioritization process with a clear understanding of the importance and potential value of each product or feature that the team intends to work on. Through the prioritization process, product managers constantly narrow down ideas to a select few they want to build and test — and they need to be confident that those ideas have the best chances of meeting your user needs and business goals.

The Output

The artifacts produced during product discovery depend on the scope and nature of the project. Sometimes it's a few sketches on the back of a napkin that a developer uses to start prototyping; sometimes it's a big PowerPoint document summarizing the process and key takeaways in an effort to bring senior executives along for the ride.

Regardless of the actual output, at the end of the process you should be able to answer the following questions with ease:

- What is the problem we are trying to solve?

- For whom are we solving it? Why should they care?

- What's the vision for the solution?

- What's in it for us?

- What's our implementation plan?

In some organizations it helps to put together a **strategic product plan** that clearly communicates the product/market fit idea by identifying:

- The product (what's the value proposition?)

- The market (what's the customer profile?)

- The fit (what's the size of the opportunity, the pricing and distribution plan?)

- The initial set of priorities and success metrics (this can change over time)

The real power of the product discovery process is that it will reassure your team that you're solving the right problems for the right users. "This is all very nice," I hear you say, "but we're a fast-moving startup and we don't have time to sit around and talk." You do if the alternative is failure, brought on by an unhealthy addiction to pretty things that lead to fifteen minutes of fame, but not much else.

We're entering an interesting era in web design. Retina displays might not have mass adoption yet, but it's only a matter of time before they become the norm. We're also seeing a level of interest in typography and graphics last experienced when color CRT monitors became a thing. There are many shiny objects out there, and if we focus on those (or on impressing the VCs who are focused on them) to the neglect of usefulness, we might find ourselves in a situation similar to that of only a few years ago, when we built Flash intros on every site just because we could.

In other words, product discovery is essential for startups precisely because we're in a time of such exciting visual innovation. We cannot let the allure of the visual tear us too far away from the usefulness of the products we develop. It is true that failure teaches us a great deal about what works and what doesn't. But it's so much cheaper and more effective to fail at a variety of ideas on paper than it is to fail at one full-blown, VC-backed idea.

Together, we can avoid building digital Brasílias — projects that generate buzz, but don't meet the needs of the people who live there. So let's discover before we build. ✍

CASE STUDY:

The User Experience Of kalahari.com

When I arrived at kalahari.com in December 2010 the site hadn't seen any significant UI improvements during the more than ten years of its existence. My job description was pretty straightforward: do something about that.

I'd like to talk about the work our team did in the first twelve months to improve the user experience of kalahari.com[73]. When I look at the site now I still see so much wrong with it — there were way too many things that we needed to fix. So this isn't an attempt to hold up our work as some kind of standard. I'm doing this in the interest of sharing our methods and the lessons learned from the trenches of real-life product management.

If you stepped through the site back in 2010 then you probably would have felt as overwhelmed as I did. Where do we start? What order should we do things in? After the first few days of having too much coffee and talking to people all over the organization, I realized that we had two primary challenges:

1. **No formal prioritization or product development process**
It was the same situation I've seen many times before. Requirements went straight from the business to develop-

---

73. http://www.kalahari.com

ers. That kicked off an endless back and forth about what was needed, with only a cursory nod to design. The first in, first out approach to prioritization was also quite common. The result was, well, not ideal. We needed to fix this.

2. **No formal user experience design**

This was no surprise, and it was the reason I took the job in the first place. There was no user research, no content strategy, no interaction design, and no visual design beyond marketing and merchandizing materials. This is the part that really excited me: the opportunity to introduce user experience design into an organization that was (to their enormous credit) hungry for it but didn't know where to start.

So we immediately got to work on both those problems.

Hello, I'm A Product Manager

Introducing a product management layer into an organization that's used to working without it is tricky. If you do it wrong it can become a political nightmare and end up ruining your chances of shipping anything worthwhile. You might have the best of intentions, but there is always the danger that the only thing people will think when they look at a product manager is, "Hey, I used to be responsible for that stuff, buddy!"

We certainly didn't make this transition perfectly, but I believe the key is to make sure that you talk to as many people as possible about what their organizational issues are, and how they think it can be done better. You have to take the time to explain the benefits of having a product team to take responsibility for strategy, vision, and execution of a product (and take the fall if it fails). And then, most importantly, you have to make the development process fair.

We now had a team of product managers who were responsible for delivering measurable business results through product solutions that met both market needs and company goals. They worked closely with their teams to develop the strategy and vision for their products. They ensured that designers and developers were included throughout the process. And most importantly: they made sure we shipped.

Hello, I'm A User Experience Designer

I knew that we needed to build a great team if we were going to follow a user-centered approach to identifying and addressing the main issues on the kalahari.com site. But building a team takes time and money, and it's hard to justify a large headcount request before you've proven that you can have a real impact on the business.

So we started small. I fulfilled the UX design role, and we hired one visual designer since that was the primary need at that stage. Then we got stuck in. On a site of this size, and with the pressure we had to make improvements quickly, we decided on a dual approach:

1. Make some initial and obvious changes to the visual design to improve hierarchy and the general aesthetic.

2. At the same time, work on a long-term UX strategy to address some of the more fundamental user experience issues on the site.

The goal was to show quickly that we knew what we were doing, and then use those successes to build out the team further and attack the areas where we could have the biggest effect on conversion rates.

Building A Roadmap

We started this process with a small team of three product managers and two designers, so we didn't initially have the luxury of user research and a long period of product discovery to build out a roadmap. Instead, we went offsite for a day and built a customer journey map for our different user journeys. It was a great way to focus on what the core experience was that we need to improve.

We also went a bit further. Based on a heuristic evaluation of the site, we annotated each step in the user journey with the obvious improvements we could make. This gave us a flexible framework for the year, and guided our roadmap throughout.

We decided early on to realign, not redesign. Our approach was to make relentless incremental progress as opposed to doing a six to nine-month project with a big bang release. Our goal was to release every three to four weeks, depending on the size of the project.

In our first two releases we took care of some basics. These changes had exactly the desired effect. User response was immediate and universally positive. In combination with some good specials, traffic started to increase. And most importantly, we were able to start growing our team to add designers, a researcher, and a front-end developer. Game on.

We spent the rest of the year systematically working through our customer experience map, starting with the most important areas where improved UX can have the biggest effects (registration, checkout, product details page, and so on). We were also able to remain flexible and shift priorities as necessary (business needs, competitor pressure, for example).

We made quite a few mistakes before hitting our stride. Sometimes we estimated the scope of work incorrectly, or we tried the wrong solution first, or we were so pressured for time that we just couldn't deliver the quality we wanted. But we dealt with each of those issues immediately and honestly. We owned our failures, we explained our frustration with arbitrary timelines, we showed how changing priorities affects costs because of the amount of time that ends up being wasted on rework (or work that never gets used). We also showed how following an approach of iterative design and development resulted in increased revenue in our key flows. Eventually our process found a good rhythm towards the middle of the year.

- Define the area we're working on, and define what success looks like (what are the metrics we're trying to improve?).

- Work in small teams of PMs, designers, and developers to sketch out new flows and develop wireframes.

- Test prototypes with users, utilizing the RITE method so that the outcome is improved designs, not PowerPoint decks with recommendations.

- Refine the designs as they evolve into high-fidelity visual designs (with more user testing as required), and deliver high-quality HTML and CSS as the final output.

The outcome was a site that was drastically different from where it was a year before, with real improvements in the success metrics we set for ourselves (positive changes in conversion of registration, checkout, and other flows).

My biggest regret about that year is that we couldn't do more. We made some great improvements to the site, but it was still so far from where it needed to be. And I know everyone on the team felt this way. We set out to build a culture of quality above all else, and it physically hurt when we had to make compromises and do something that was counter to that culture. But it certainly was a great start. ❧

CHAPTER 4:

Product Roadmaps

The Importance Of Product Roadmaps

We've covered a lot of ground on product planning and prioritization. We've generated some good ideas along the way. So, now what? Should you create a product roadmap? Those have fallen out of fashion over the last few years, particularly in more agile-minded organizations like Basecamp, with Jason Fried proclaiming[74]:

> *Instead of the roadmap, just look out a few weeks at a time. Work on the next most important thing. What's the point of a long list when you can't work on everything at once anyway? Finish what's important now and then figure out what's important next. One step at a time.*

It's hard to disagree with a person (and a company) you have great admiration for, as I do for Jason and Basecamp. But I do think it's important to set the record straight on product roadmaps — particularly when it comes to large organizations. Jason's article highlights two main concerns with product roadmaps, that summarize the general concern you often hear about it:

---

74. "Product roadmaps are dangerous" – http://smashed.by/product-roadmaps

- Product roadmaps assume you know what's going to happen 6–18 months from now.

- Product roadmaps set expectations, so you can't change them (and if you do change them it becomes a worthless exercise).

My purpose here is not to disagree with Jason in particular, but to use his argument to make some general points about the importance of roadmaps. So let's look at each of these points in turn.

PRODUCT ROADMAPS ASSUME YOU KNOW THE FUTURE

Jason writes:

> When you let a product roadmap guide you you let the past drive the future. You're saying "6 months ago I knew what 18 months from now would look like." You're saying "I'm not going to pay attention to now, I'm going to pay attention to then." You're saying "I should be working at the Psychic Friends Network."

This is not what a product roadmap is, or what it's supposed to do. The purpose of a product roadmap is to set out a long-term vision for the business, and break that up into smaller, meaningful pieces of work, based on what you know now. It's a fallacy that this is an unchangeable list of dates about where the business is headed. A product roadmap that doesn't react to day-to-day changes in the market and within the company is a pretty dumb document.

At organizations where I've been responsible for the roadmap we've always been very clear that it is a flexible guideline that can (and must) change frequently as needed. It is not always easy to convince teams to see roadmaps in this flexible way, but it's worth the effort. The trick is not to describe the flexible roadmap in a way that makes it sound like an excuse to be indecisive and not committing to everything. Instead, point out that a flexible roadmap is the only way to remain proactive when important changes happen in the company or the external landscape, while also keeping your eye on the product's vision and goals.

Roadmaps like these give teams and managers realistic goals to work towards. It's a common vision, a sense of direction that's more than just fluffy language — it's concrete evidence that we're headed somewhere good, and we know how to get there.

We can change direction as many times as we want. This doesn't make it a useless exercise: it means that instead of starting fresh on a new roadmap every few weeks, you build on your past successes, don't make the same mistakes twice, and keep making measurable progress since you can see where you came from.

PRODUCT ROADMAPS SET THE WRONG EXPECTATIONS

Jason writes further in his article:

> The other problem with roadmaps is the expectations game. People expect you to deliver what you say you will in 4, 5, 6 months. And what if you have a better idea?

What if there's a shift in the market that you need to address? What if what you thought wasn't what actually happened? Any change in the roadmap nullifies the roadmap. Then the map isn't a map at all.

If you have this problem it doesn't mean that product roadmaps are wrong: it means that you're doing it wrong. As long as everyone in the organization buys into the fluid nature of the roadmap, you won't have this problem. In an organization where I once worked we did this mainly through the mechanism of what we called the product council (I was partial to Intergalactic Product Force, but for some reason that didn't fly so well). Here's how it works.

The product council is made up of the VPs of every department in the organization: engineering, marketing, support, category, and so on. This body has a weekly meeting where we discuss the current product roadmap and priorities. We ask ourselves if we're still working on the most important things. If something more important comes up, we prioritize it higher in the roadmap, and something else shifts down; if we're happy with the direction, we do nothing. If a new opportunity arises we ask ourselves, "Is this more important than what we're working on right now? Or is this something we should work on next? If so, what moves down the priority list?"

From here, I communicated with my product team about any changes, and we discussed this to make sure no one missed anything. But then — and this is important — the product managers had complete autonomy and ownership over the implementation of the roadmap. The product council sets the priorities (with input from all parts of the organization), but the product managers work with their development teams (and others) to set the timeline, the implementation details, the design, everything.

How the product council could work

This process has three main advantages. First, it gives the management team complete transparency into what the product team is working on, and it allows anyone to make the case for a change in priorities. This transparency takes away the vast majority of the politics you see in many organizations, and it frees up the teams to do what they do best — execute.

Second, it prevents scope creep. Nothing can go on the roadmap without something else moving out or down. As anyone who has ever worked at a large organization knows, this is a critical part of a successful development cycle.

Finally, it gives the product manager and their teams what they need to be successful: direction and autonomy. As Jocelyn Glei said[75]: "Give your team members what they need to thrive, and then get out of the way."

WHY PRODUCT ROADMAPS ARE SAFE (AND ESSENTIAL)

At a practical level I went through the exercise of figuring out how we could execute in an organization without a roadmap. And although it might work in some circumstances, in general it seems to me like a very dangerous proposition. Changes to current pages and flows affect changes we'll make down the line — the product manager has to think about that.

If you're serious about frequent incremental change as opposed to large redesign projects, you can't live without a roadmap because you'll have no idea how far you've gone, what you still need to do, and what's more important than something else. And perhaps most dangerous of all, everyone in the organization will come to you and want all their projects done right now, and you'll have no systematic method for dealing with that in a way that's

---

75. "What Motivates Us To Do Great Work?" – http://smashed.by/motivate

best for the business. Andy Wagner summed up my feelings on this issue quite succinctly in a comment on Jason's 37signals post[76]:

> [Product roadmaps are] an opportunity to dream about what the future might look like so that as you make your day-to-day responses to the customer, you can do so consistent with building the future state. It emphatically should **not** be anything to be [a] slave to, it should be dynamic and notional, not static and specific.

Jason wrote, "The further you get from now, the less you know. And the less you know, the worse your decisions will be." We agree on that. My argument is that without a roadmap you only see now. And if you only see now without seeing yesterday and tomorrow, you don't see a whole lot. And "the less you know, the worse your decisions will be."

The Elements Of A Roadmap

So what does a product roadmap look like? Again, that completely depends on what the organization is comfortable with. My preferred way to communicate a roadmap is as lightweight as possible — whiteboards in the office, or company wikis. It's dangerous to introduce documents and internal systems that people aren't used to, so wherever people are already working, use that platform. Many

---

76. http://smashed.by/roadmaps-comment

organizations already have an internal wiki, so that's a good place to start.

It's also very important to make roadmaps as visible as possible to the rest of the company. We'll discuss this more when we talk about functional specifications, but product managers work out in the open. And they do this because their goal isn't personal glory; their goal is a great product. For that to happen they can't be precious about their ideas, and they can't run the risk of doing things in secret that could hurt the product or backfire on them politically. That's another reason why whiteboards are great at communicating roadmaps — everyone can see them and comment on the ideas and progress.

In my view, product roadmaps should contain the following elements:

- The priority of the project (1 being the highest priority, all the way down).

- A summary of no more than ten words.

- A detailed description of no more than fifty words.

- A list of contacts involved in the project (PM, business, development lead).

- An indication of the business impact and the estimated level of effort.

- A link to the functional specification as soon as it's available.

You'll notice there's something conspicuously missing from this list: *dates*. This might be controversial, but I believe that product roadmaps shouldn't have dates associated with projects, only priorities. That's where my views start to converge with Jason's general principle in his post — work on the most important thing until it's done, and then move on to the next thing, and the next. Here's an example of what a flexible roadmap could look like, including the elements mentioned above:

High Level Product Priorities - 2010 Q4

- Legend
- Buyer
- Search and Backoffice
- eContent, Mobile, APIs
- Seller
- Customer journey

Legend

★ - in progress
⚠ - Problems - attention required
✔ - Completed

Buyer

Priority	Status	Summary	Detail	Business	PM	Dev lead	Business impact	Effort	Spec
	✔	Visual refresh of header/footer	Visual changes to the header and footer, as well as changes to reduce rounded corners and replace buttons	Rian	Rian	Anthony/Dylan	Low	Low	Wiki
1	★	Credit card immediate settlements	Immediate settlement for credit cards – automatic on hold for foreign orders + automated fraud checker in real time	Gary	Hein	Garth	High	High	BUYE?
2	★	Replatforming interface	Frontend and platform work for replatforming (Framework, Header/Footer, Home, Product pages, SRP, etc.)	Mike N	Hein/Rian		High	High	
2	★	Visual refresh phase 2	Global font change, one-colour banners, left nav changes, replace old promo block	Rian	Hein	Lorinda	Medium	Medium	BUYE?
2		Checkout redesign	Redesign of checkout pages, limited to the pages themselves (no combining of pages or flow changes)	Rian	Hein		High	High	BUYE?
2		Login/registration redesign	Redesign of login/registration page	Rian	Hein		Medium	Medium	BUYE?
3		New eTrader platform	Redesign of affiliates site, including required interfaces with Hybris/Endeca/SAP	Liz					
3		Profile page redesign	Redesign of Profile page, including rewrite of copy	Rian	Hein		Medium	Medium	

Example of a flexible roadmap with priorities but no dates (Larger view[77])

---

77. http://smashed.by/roadmap

Of course, it's impossible to get rid of dates completely, so
I prefer to do that in the release schedule. This schedule
lists the dates when the company plans to release code
(often in two- or three-week intervals if the company uses
agile methodologies), and indicates what projects are
scheduled to go live on each date. This might sound like
just another document to maintain, but it allows you to
remain flexible with the schedule. Code release dates
might not change, but which projects and features go into each release can. If something goes wrong, or too
many corners need to get cut, a project can be moved to
the next release date without changing its priority or
compromising on quality just to hit an arbitrary date.
Here's an example of what such a release schedule could
look like:

Product Roadmap - Release Schedule FY2013

	Date	Sprint	Product	Major features
✓	February 9, 2012	Sprint 12	Buyer	Better solution for large images on PDP SEO improvements Improvements to Contact Us flow Marketing enhancements for social sharing Bug fixes
✓	March 6, 2012	Sprint 13	Buyer	SEO improvements Remove Stationary from site Introduce estimated delivery dates for open orders Bug fixes
	April 24, 2012	Sprint 14	Buyer	Change messaging for Marketplace delivery time SEO improvements Bug fixes
	May 17, 2012	Sprint 15	Buyer	Move mini-basket into header Improvements to Newsletter subscription management Librarybox enhancements to Help information Remove eMagazines from site
	June 7, 2012	Sprint 16	Buyer	Full-width home page & shop pages Add TV license capture in Checkout Move momentum multipy to voucher back model
	June 28, 2012	Sprint 17	Buyer	Full-width search results page Help page rewrite

Example release schedule with dates and features within the release
(Larger view[78])

Coming up next...

With your strategic product plan in place, as well as a roadmap and tentative release schedule to guide your steps, it's time to start executing and ship stuff.

We've discussed the product planning phase of product management in isolation, but of course that's not how it works in practice. Everything mentioned in part 1 of this book happens continuously as the product evolves. But as important as planning is, you can't just do that forever — where's the fun in that? And that's where Part 3 comes in. Let's talk about product execution — the process of validating your ideas with customers, and building those ideas out in the most effective way. ❧

---

78. http://smashed.by/release

Part 3: Execution

CHAPTER 5:

Defining A Product

In the first half of this book we spent a lot of time discussing why product management is important, what product managers are like, and how to make sure you spend time building the right products for the right people. That was time well spent, because as we've talked about at length, it's way more expensive to build the wrong product than it is to find out early in the design and development process that you're not quite hitting the mark. Now that we've discussed how ongoing product planning works, and how to create a strategic product plan, it's time to focus on the process of execution.

In this section we'll discuss the various activities that go into getting a product live, and how to work with different teams to accomplish your goals. We'll also briefly discuss the process of user-centered design, which is an essential component throughout the execution process to ensure that the organization remains market-driven. PMs should make sure the user experience teams are always involved in the process. Even if a PM doesn't perform all the activities of user-centered design themselves, it is important to understand the process and use the output in decision-making.

Below is a diagram that shows the outline of this section:

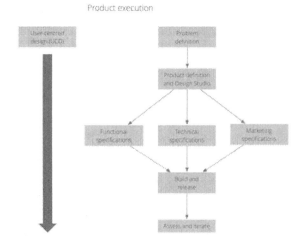

The product execution process

We'll start with a discussion of problem and product definitions, and how they're different from functional and
technical specifications. We'll then take a detour to talk
about user-centered design and the importance of prototype testing with target users, and then apply those principles to the rest of the process — building and releasing
features, and assessing their success.

Problem Definition

Requirements often get a bad rap, especially in the context of lean principles and agile development, where it is
assumed that defining requirements is about figuring out
what features stakeholders think should be in a product

before you start designing and building. That might be how requirements were viewed in traditional waterfall processes, but it's not a good way to build product. I always picture a product manager with lab coat and clipboard, walking around the office asking random people what features they want a product to have. It might seem like collaboration, but that approach is mostly about politics — making everyone feel like they've had input. Collaboration is essential, but we've already discussed the best ways to build collaboration into the process. Traditional requirements gathering is way too focused on features, and very rarely takes user needs into account. So, instead, we need to define requirements a little differently. With that in mind, I'm going to refer to this part of the process as the problem definition phase instead.

It's important to differentiate between a problem definition and a specification. A problem definition is a short statement of the problem you're trying to solve. A specification explains how to solve the problem. If the product planning section taught us anything, it's the importance of keeping the problem you're solving front and center at all times. That's why it's so important to break up ideas into problem definitions first, before starting to work on solutions (or hypotheses in the context of lean methodologies), so that you don't lose sight of the problem that's being solved.

A good way to write problem definitions is to use a format similar to user stories in agile development. I call these problem stories: *[user] has [problem] when [trigger]*. For example, a PM on a financial services product might have a problem definition that states: "Investors are not able to submit supporting documents online when they need to make changes to client portfolios." That becomes a statement of the problem that needs to be solved through product improvements. The addition of the trigger element also ensures that you remain focused on the cause of the action that users need to take to find the product useful.

An effective problem definition includes the following elements:

- It clearly defines target users (the target users can also be the business or the development team).

- It clearly defines the problem that needs to be solved.

- It clearly defines under what circumstances the problem occurs (the trigger events).

- It has enough supporting documentation to provide context on the target users and the problem to guide the design of the solution.

To reiterate, this phase isn't about making a list of what everyone in the office wants to see in a new product. But that is unfortunately what often happens — everyone gets in a room and rambles off their wish lists for what features should be in a product, based on their own feelings and preferences. Then the poor product manager has to sort through all of that and create a coherent product.

No. Let's stop this crazy behavior. Instead, let's work on providing a clear definition of a manageable problem to solve for a specific set of users, and then spend our time creating the right solutions.

Where do these problem definitions come from? Well, that should be very easy at this point — your problem definitions are pulled from the prioritized list of needs (user, business, and technical), as laid out in the strategic product plan. For example, if the next high priority project is a redesign of an e-commerce account or profile section, the PM would take all the background from the product planning phase and distill that into a simple problem story, like this:

> *Buyers can't find the information they're looking for when they want to check on the status of their orders.*

This problem story forms the basis of the project that anchors everyone on the user, the problem, and the product context.

Product Definition And Design Studio

Once you've selected a problem definition to work on in a specific project, it's time to come up with possible solutions for the identified problems. Here the team spends time creating product ideas. This is similar to what the lean movement refers to as forming hypotheses — formulating assumptions or ideas with the goal of testing those ideas through user research.

In chapter 3 about product discovery I talked about the importance of variation before an iterative process starts. If the team has done a bunch of thinking and sketching during discovery, use those ideas as a starting point to formalize possible solutions in the form of prototypes that can be tested and validated with potential users before they're built. I've mostly used Axure RP[79] to create interactive prototypes, but there are plenty of other tools and frameworks available for prototyping, from code-specific solutions (ZURB Foundation[80], Bootstrap[81]) to linking paper prototypes together (POP for iPhone[82]). The type of prototype doesn't matter as much as it has to be realistic enough to get real user feedback on. In general, static wireframes are not that useful, since they don't allow for user interaction, and they're also not very helpful as a way for developers to figure out what the product does (unless you spend a lot of time annotating the wireframes, which isn't a very good use of time).

It is often not feasible to go out and test a bunch of prototype solutions to the same problem, so in those cases it is useful to create several variations as a team, and then narrow down to one or two solutions to be validated in usability tests.

An effective way to do this is to run a design studio with the project team. A design studio workshop gets an entire team involved in the design process to develop and refine ideas in a short amount of time — often within a few hours. Design studio should include team members across the organization: designers, content strategists, developers, product managers, marketers, and so on. There

---

79. http://www.axure.com/
80. http://foundation.zurb.com/
81. http://getbootstrap.com/
82. https://popapp.in/

are many different ways to run a design studio workshop, but there are usually some common elements.

Start with a discussion about the problem definition you're working on, so that everyone has a common understanding of the focus area and the personas you intend to solve the problem for. Then proceed through three (or more) sketching iterations, using the same process with every cycle: sketch, present, critique, refine.

- Iteration 1: Sketch individually using a six-up template (six variations per page).

- Present to the team, get critique.

- Iteration 2: Pick the best idea, sketch a refined concept individually using a one-up template (only one variation per page).

- Present to the team, get critique.

- Iteration 3: Pick the two to three best ideas, sketch one refined concept as a team using large pieces of paper.

Since quite a bit of critique happens during design studio, it's important to make sure the group knows how to give good feedback. I discussed good critique in detail in Part 1, so I won't rehash it here, except to highlight the important components that should be reiterated during each design studio session:

- Let each person explain their sketch or idea in full.

- The team should first point out what they like about the sketch, so that the presenter knows which directions to pursue.

- Phrase critique as questions to give the presenter a chance to respond and explain the reasoning behind their decisions.

At the end of this process you'll have a small number of ideas that are ready for prototyping and testing with users. You'll also be comfortable that you tried many different variations in a short period of time, and refined those ideas into what you believe solves the problem in the best possible way. Now it's time to get your target users involved, so let's talk about that within the context of user-centered design. ❧

CHAPTER 6:

User-Centered Design And Workflows

Usability testing has always been a cornerstone of my product work. My road to product manager started in the user experience research team at eBay, so I look at most product work through a user-centered design lens. As I moved into an agency role later in my career, things got a bit tricky. It turns out that usability testing is a difficult thing to sell to clients. The same concerns always come up: it will take too long, ten tests aren't enough, and the rest. But I learned to keep pushing, and stood firm on not taking on a project if it didn't include usability testing. I soon realized something very important. Clients fight against usability testing only until they observe their first one. Then the light goes on, and they start throwing buckets of money at us (OK, not really, but that would be nice). It only takes seeing one user struggle with your product to see the value of usability testing.

Considering how essential this topic is, I'd like to take a slight detour in this chapter to discuss UCD in a bit more detail. This isn't a separate step in the product development process. Rather, it is a methodology that should accompany and guide the process from start to finish. It makes sense to address it at this point because as you get into the execution phase of building a product, UCD becomes increasingly important to ensure you don't just build blindly into the night, but test your ideas with real target market users.

The value of user experience design has been discussed in detail elsewhere, so I'll assume a basic understanding of the value of good design, and that we all want a good experience in our products. In short, we want to create products that are useful, usable, and delightful. And we want to integrate that with what's technically possible, what's profitable, and what fits with our strategic goals. That's what UCD aims to accomplish.

There is one benefit of UCD in particular that I'd like to focus on here, and that is that the methodology helps organizations spend less time on building the wrong stuff. Following a user-centered design process drastically reduces development and maintenance costs. C. Karat points out[83]:

> *Eighty percent of software lifecycle costs occur after the product is released, in the maintenance phase. Of that work, 80% is due to unmet or unseen user requirements and only 20% is due to bugs or reliability problems.*

And Albert Lederer and Jayesh Prasad found the following[84]:

---

83. Karat, C., "Usability engineering in dollars and cents," Software, IEEE , vol. 10, no.3, pp. 88, 89, May 1993.
84. Albert L. Lederer and Jayesh Prasad, "Nine management guidelines for better cost estimating," *Commun. ACM* 35, 2 (February 1992), 51-59. (http://smashed.by/cost-estimating)

63% of software projects exceed their budget estimates, with the top four reasons all relating to product usability: frequent requests for changes by users, overlooked tasks, users' lack of understanding of their own requirements, and insufficient user analysis communication and understanding.

In *Cost-Justifying Usability*[85] the authors point out that if the cost of making design changes during the user-centered design phase is taken as the baseline, the same changes would cost ten times as much during the development phase, and a hundred times as much after the product is released.

So, the earlier you discover needs and problems, the more money you save on development. It makes sense, and yet it's still harder to convince organizations (and sometimes even ourselves) to do things right the first time, than it is to convince them to do it over when something fails. This doesn't mean that the product has to be perfect and complete from day one. But it does mean that instead of dealing with a misfire in terms of user needs, you have a good baseline to iterate from.

The most compelling argument[86] comes from Marty Cagan, who says:

Instead of using one prototyper for a few weeks, [most organizations] use the full engineering team for full release cycles to build the software that is then QA'ed and

---

85. *Cost-Justifying Usability*, Randolph G. Bias (Editor), Deborah J. Mayhew, 1994, Academic Press.
86. "Product Discovery" – http://smashed.by/product-discovery

deployed into production systems. This is why it typically takes so many companies three or more releases over one to two years to get something usable and useful. They are using the engineering organization to build a very, very expensive prototype, and they use their live customers as unwitting test subjects.

UCD is a well-established approach that creates more successful products by making sure that we design for user needs, not our own whims and desires. It is an iterative approach that saves costs by making sure we test our ideas with users before they go into production. UCD is based on a few key steps, all linked to the three classes of research we discussed in chapter 2 on user needs:

- **Step 1: Understand needs.** Start with *exploratory research* to uncover the most important unmet user needs to address with the product.

- **Step 2: Create concepts and/or prototypes.** Create sketches and prototypes to make ideas tangible without tying up expensive development time.

- **Step 3: Test with users and iterate.** Run usability tests on the concepts and prototypes with five to ten target users to validate the ideas and uncover usability issues (*design research*). Go back to step 2 and repeat as many times as needed or possible.

- **Step 4: Launch and measure.** Develop the product, launch, and measure the impact it has on predefined metrics (*assessment research*). Combine with design research methods to uncover why the metrics have moved up or down. Make changes as needed.

It's also important to highlight one of the best things about UCD: it shrinks to fit. If you don't have a lot of time or budget, you can still do a scaled down version of each of the steps in the process.

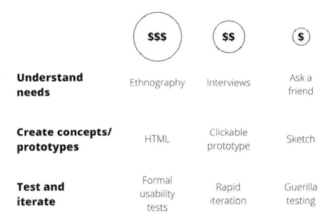

User-centered design shrinks to fit any budget or timeline

There have been some critiques of user-centered design in recent times, and some arguments that we need to start using other design methodologies, such as activity-centered design (ACD)[87], alongside (or instead of) UCD. Cennydd Bowles sums up the argument against UCD

---

87. For a good overview of ACD, see "Stop Designing for Users" by Mike Long – http://smashed.by/stop-designing-users

well in his article "Looking Beyond User-Centered Design[88]". Issues include the fact that it takes longer than other methodologies, it doesn't always take a designer's visual style in consideration, and it can sometimes be misunderstood as science that leads to certainty (which it is not).

As with most things, the methodology needs to fit the task. In some cases UCD might not be the best fit, but in a majority of projects I've worked on, it is the best methodology we have to make sure we design useful, usable products.

Despite its many advantages it can sometimes be difficult to introduce UCD into an organization. When we run into obstacles we often blame the organization for being behind the times, or not understanding why it's important to invest in good design. But shifting the blame is the wrong approach to take. The onus is on us to prove, within our industry and the companies we work at, that good design will result in positive return on investment.

If I remember one thing from Marketing 101, it's this obvious but often forgotten truth: businesses exist to make a profit. Companies work hard to make us happy for one reason only: so we will buy more of their stuff. This seems obvious, but it's important to remember. Because when you talk to the management teams of your organization, telling them how beautiful their site will be once you're done with it is just not going to cut it.

To prove the value of user-centered design you have to prove that by investing in it, the business will make more

---

88. "Looking Beyond User-Centered Design" – http://smashed.by/beyond

money. It's as simple as that. Well, the concept is simple. The execution is... complicated. I'd like to propose some ways to help us prove the value of design, so that we can spend more of our time building great experiences and less time telling people why they should build great experiences.

Proving that good design will make your organization or client more money is not something you can express in a formula and do overnight. It involves some hard work and clever thinking (time well spent) to figure out what works best for the context you're designing in. In some cases, like designing a checkout process, it is relatively easy to define success metrics, benchmark, and show that a redesign resulted in more money — because checkout is where the money is.

In other cases, for flows that are further removed from direct revenue generation, it can be much harder to find the money link. In those cases, a conversion model is often the right way to go:

In most online user flows you can make a strong case that an improved conversion rate (or reduced drop-off rate) will result in increased revenue. Once that link is made, what remains is to prove that an improved user experience results in improved conversion rates. But there are immediately two challenges with this approach:

- How do you buy the time you need to prove that UX works?

- How do you find the right conversion rate model to link UX to conversion rates (and ultimately revenue)?

So let's dive into that.

Buying Time To Do The Right Thing

Getting an organization or client to spend time doing UCD can be quite tricky in the beginning. Without real data, it's hard to show the value. But without the time to do the process right, it's hard to get real data. And so the vicious circle continues.

One way to buy some time is to show case studies where an investment in UCD has resulted in significant revenue lifts. One of these case studies is Jared Spool's $300 million button, where a simple design change resulted in an enormous revenue lift. Spool writes[89]:

> When the team contacted us, they'd already pretty much decided what the problem was and how they were going to fix it, even though they had never watched any shoppers make purchases. And they were dead wrong. Not only was their fix not going to help, our research showed that it was going to increase abandonment.
>
> Two weeks of usability testing on the live site (and on competitors' sites), followed by two weeks of iterative paper prototype testing produced a streamlined check-

89. "UIEtips: The $300 Million Button" – http://smashed.by/300-million

out process, which, once implemented, showed a dra-
matic increase in revenues. It's amazing what you'll
learn when you actually watch your users.

In another example, Airbnb changed the way to add prop-
erties to a wish list from a star to a heart, which resulted
in a 30% increase in engagement[90]. And when Veeam
Software changed some link text from "Request a quote"
to "Request pricing", its click-through rate increased by
161%[91].

Obviously not all UX changes are going to have this
much impact. But sharing stories like this with senior
management should help to make the case for investing
in a proper user-centered design process. I know this is
easier said than done, but mountains can be moved with
some solid data and stubborn persistence.

So, let's assume you've shown that a good UX can increase revenue quite significantly. How do you go about
proving it for one of your own projects?

The Three 'A's

One marketing principle quite useful for UCD is to view
the revenue as coming from one or more of three sources:

- **Acquisition**: getting new users to sign up for your site or
  service

---

90. "How Airbnb Evolved To Focus On Social Rather Than Searches" –
    http://smashed.by/airbnb
91. "How changing a single word increased click through rate by 161%" –
    http://smashed.by/click-through

- **Activation**: getting those new users to make their first purchase

- **Activity**: getting those first-time purchasers to come back for more

If you can tie a UCD project to one or more of these sources of revenue by showing that you increased conversion rates in those areas, you'll have what you need. You'd have shown that design equals money. Here are some hypothetical examples:

- A *registration flow redesign* can be shown to improve conversion from sign-up landing page to signed-up users. This ties into acquisition.

- Improvements to a *search results page* can be shown to improve conversions from search to items placed in a shopping cart. This ties into activation and activity.

- *Home page layout and content changes* can be shown to improve click-through rates on merchandising offers specific to new users. This ties into activation.

And this list can go on and on. It won't always be easy, but every UCD project should be measurable in terms of its impact on the business; tying it to one of the three 'A's is a good structured way of anchoring all design changes in business goals and, ultimately, revenue. Define your success metrics, benchmark those metrics before any changes are made, and then measure the (hopefully improved) increase in metrics.

Designers need to assume some of the blame for often having to fight very hard for appropriate resources to do our jobs. We need to understand why businesses exist, and follow a strategic approach to proving the ROI of design.

- Show historical case studies to buy some time and resources to follow a proper UCD process on one or more of your projects.

- Start on a project where changes can be measured by an improvement in one of the three 'A's of revenue generation: acquisition, activation, and activity.

- Benchmark well before the start of the project, follow through on the UCD commitment, and measure your results[92].

This process should give product managers the opportunity to introduce user-centered design into an organization in a measured and responsible way. ❧

92. See this post on Six Revisions for some tips on which measurement tools to use: "How to Measure the Effectiveness of Web Designs" – http://smashed.by/effectiveness

What About Responsive Design?

Workflows: Making UCD Part Of Every Project

One of the big open questions in the design community is how to make user-centered design part of our workflows in an increasingly multi-device world. This isn't a book about responsive design — there are plenty of those to go around — but I do think it's important to address some possible workflows for product managers to ensure that projects incorporate user-centered design while also acknowledging the progress of web development. Here is a workflow that works well in the agency I worked at:

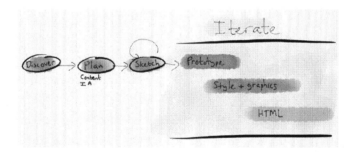

The goal of this approach is to stay grounded in two core principles:

1. **Content first.** We need to stop thinking about content in terms of layout, and plan content independent of design.

2. **Mobile first.** We need to stop the focus on device-specific thinking, and assume a multi-device world where we work on style direction independent of layout.

I'll briefly go through each step in the diagram and how it helps us to accomplish these goals.

During discovery we research to uncover user needs, develop personas, and create the user journey map that becomes our product strategy; we discussed this in detail in part 2 of the book.

In the planning phase we evolve the user journey map into a content plan and information architecture document; we discussed this in part 2 as well. Once we have our scaffolding in place, we start the design process.

We rarely do static wireframes any more, but we do a lot of sketching. The benefits of sketching have been proven time and time again. What I like most about the sketching process is how it allows the team to try multiple solutions to a problem, before settling on one or two ideas to iterate further. I like using Zurb's responsive sketchsheets[93] as templates because they keep us focused on a multi-device approach.

Once we've gone through the sketching phase with clients, and we know what approach we'd like to pursue, we start prototyping. We mainly use Axure, but there are many solutions out there to suit a variety of approaches. Axure isn't natively responsive (yet), so we've been building two prototypes on our projects: starting mobile first; and then moving on to desktop. This isn't ideal, but it

93. "Responsive Sketchsheets" – http://smashed.by/sketchsheets

works for our current purposes. We have a strong focus on user testing, so we test these prototypes in our usability lab, and iterate the design based on the findings.

Towards the end of the prototyping process we start working on style tiles[94] so we can have a discussion about graphics with clients without focusing on layout and flow issues. Style tiles sit between mood boards and full comps in that they show fonts, colors, and interface elements such as buttons and form fields, but they're not concerned with layout very much. In recent years this method has been expanded to include ideas like style prototypes (a responsive HTML rendering of a style tile[95]), and interactive style tiles (a WordPress plugin solution for style tiles[96]).

We've seen huge success with this approach. Once clients are comfortable with the visual direction, the focus can return to discussing how the UI will help them meet their business goals and user needs. It also makes the move from prototype to graphic design much smoother.

94. Style Tiles – http://styletil.es/
95. "Our New Responsive Design Deliverable: The Style Prototype" – http://smashed.by/style-prototype
96. Interactive Style Tiles - Short Demo on Vimeo – http://smashed.by/interactive-style-tiles

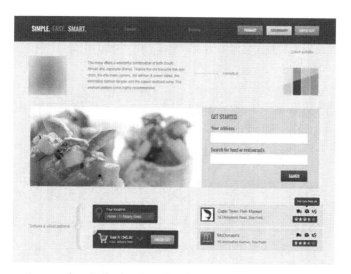

*An example style tile, showing colors, buttons, fields, and font choices
(Style tile by Alex Maughan[97])*

There is some concern that style tiles shortchange clients because they don't show a holistic view of the canvas[98], which is why we're not completely post-PSD[99] yet — but we definitely don't create the entire site in Photoshop. Since we have an interactive prototype and strong style guides, we generally only create about six or so pages in Photoshop, so clients can get a good feel for the direction (and that holistic canvas). Since clients are already so familiar with the site by the time they see Photoshop comps, they are generally totally fine with only seeing a few pages, and doing the rest of the work in code.

97. http://maughan.me/
98. See "Designing In The Transition To A Multi-Device World" by Francisco Inchauste – http://smashed.by/multi-device
99. "The Post-PSD Era" – http://smashed.by/post-psd

By the time we jump into Photoshop we've generally already started working on front-end development. We build the components of the framework using the prototype and style tiles, and pick up speed as the graphic design gets finalized. We don't use boilerplate frameworks like Foundation and Bootstrap for production code. On this point we stand with Aaron Gustafson[100]:

> I find Foundation, Bootstrap, and similar frameworks interesting from an educational standpoint, but I would never use one when building a production site. For prototyping a concept, sure, but to take one of these into production you need to be rigorous in your removal of unused CSS and JavaScript or you end up creating a heavy, slow experience for you[r] users.

An important point on the last three phases: as the diagram points out, these are all very much iterative phases. We make changes all the time based on user feedback, and discussions between designers, developers, and the client. I think we can all agree that responsive design is messy, and we just need to get comfortable with a certain amount of ambiguity during design and development. That's OK, as long as we're prepared for it.

It's been an enormous learning process — and we're still figuring out the best ways to make responsive web design our default approach. But we're committed to it, because we believe in content parity[101], and we're con-

---

100. "Responsive web design: 6 experts, 4 questions" – http://smashed.by/ rwd-experts
101. "Content Parity" – http://smashed.by/content-parity

vinced that responsive design is the approach that will get us there. Here are some things we've learned along the way.

First, you can't wing content choreography. We can't just make our front-end developers figure out what happens at each breakpoint. This is something we have to plan together to consider all the goals and constraints of the project. Breakpoint graphs are particularly helpful in this step (see Stephen Hay's book *Responsive Design Workflow*[102]).

Second, optimize for touch, and support keyboard actions. Josh Clark points out that "every desktop UI should be designed for touch now[103]." He's right. The lines are blurring between what is considered desktop and mobile, so we should just assume everything is a touchscreen, and make controls easy to discover and manipulate.

The benefits go beyond mobile. Putting mobile first helps us create better desktop sites as well, because we remain focused on meeting core user needs and ensuring there is an easy and discoverable path through the flows. There is no room for cruft on smaller screens, and that makes our desktop designs better as well.

Finally, it's hard, but it's worth it. As Ben Callahan points out in "The Responsive Dip[104]", "The fact that we don't know how to do something today doesn't mean we shouldn't strive to do it tomorrow." No one has it all fig-

102. *Responsive Design Workflow* – http://smashed.by/rwd-workflow
103. "New Rule: Every Desktop Design Has To Go Finger-Friendly" (Global Moxie) – http://smashed.by/touch-design
104. "The Responsive Dip" – http://smashed.by/responsive-dip

ured out, so I don't know about you, but I want to be part of shaping the future of the web, no matter how hard it is.

We have much maturing to do, but I'm excited about the progress we've made in shifting our entire process toward building responsive sites. Every project runs just a little bit smoother, and that's encouraging. So my only advice to those standing on the edge of responsive design is this: jump in. It's worth it. ❧

CHAPTER 7:

Specifications

It's time to discuss the part of product management that strikes fear into the heart of anyone who has worked in a large organization: the spec document. It doesn't matter what you call it — PRD, BRD, BRS — those acronyms all mean the same thing to product managers, designers, and developers alike: piles and piles of unnecessary paper. But fear not, we're going to break through the bad experiences and talk about a way to do documentation that actually helps us make better products, not make us tear our hair out.

In this chapter I'll discuss three kinds of specifications:

- Functional specifications (how the product should work).

- Technical specifications (how the product should be implemented).

- Marketing specifications (how the product should be communicated to users).

Before we continue, it's important to address the question, "Do we really need a spec?" I cannot say it better than Joel Spolsky, so I'll quote his response[105] in full:

---

105. "Painless Functional Specifications - Part 1: Why Bother?" – http://smashed.by/
functional-spec

[F]ailing to write a spec is the single biggest unnecessary risk you take in a software project. It's as stupid as setting off to cross the Mojave desert with just the clothes on your back, hoping to "wing it." Programmers and software engineers who dive into code without writing a spec tend to think they're cool gunslingers, shooting from the hip. They're not. They are terribly unproductive. They write bad code and produce shoddy software, and they threaten their projects by taking giant risks which are completely uncalled for.

Having said that, the majority of specification documents are bad. They are long, they are boring, they are done just to check a box to say they were done, they are written once and never updated, and most damningly, they don't get used during development. That is a situation product managers desperately need to avoid. If a spec isn't being used actively during development, it's not the developer's fault: it's the product manager's fault. It's up to the product manager to understand what kind of document would be useful to developers, and then provide such a document — one that is much, much better than winging it. That's what we'll focus on in this chapter.

Functional Specifications

The functional spec describes how a product works from a user's perspective. It's not focused on how it will be implemented (that's covered in the technical spec), but on defining flows and screens, and how users will experience the product. This might sound a bit academic to some, and against the spirit of the lean movement that's all about getting out of the deliverables business, but we have to remember that documentation isn't bad — bad documentation is bad. Good functional specs help teams communicate, save time, and build better products. But to make sure your functional specs fall into the good documentation category, there are a few important points to remember.

SPECS SHOULD BE DYNAMIC

They are not written once and forgotten about. This is why specs shouldn't be written in Microsoft Word (no more *v27_FINAL4.docx* file names). Instead, use collaborative tools like a wiki or Google Docs to make it easier to edit and access the most recent version.

SPECS SHOULD BE ACCESSIBLE

The spec document isn't something that the PM writes in isolation before coming down the mountain to hand over their Ten Commandments to the development team to implement. Anyone in the organization should be able to access the specs at any time, and team members should be able to ask questions and contribute to the spec. That's another reason why Word is out, and online collaborative tools are in. Seriously, uninstall Microsoft Word.

SPECS SHOULD BE FLEXIBLE

The biggest and most valid criticism of functional spec documents is that they are too rigid. Most are merely a list of requirements that were written by people far away from actual implementation, and once their job is done, they are unable to adapt in the face of reality. That's not how it should work. There is always going to be a measure of uncertainty in the functional spec, which will only become clear once development starts. This is a good thing, provided the entire team is on board with it. It means that teams can adapt to the needs of the products and users, and that they are willing to remove, change, or add features if needed (that is, if the user evidence or business need is there).

So what goes into a spec? This is the only part of the book where things might feel a little bit like a textbook. But please stick with it, because this is important, and it will make your life (and the lives of everyone who works with you) so much easier.

Here are the basic components of a good functional spec. For smaller projects you might not need all these sections, but it's still good to think about them, and use this as a basic template at the start of each project.

PROJECT SUMMARY

The project summary should be concise and to the point, while communicating enough information so that anyone in the company can take over the project if needed, and know exactly who to talk to and what needs to be done. Typically, the following pieces of information should be included.

Contacts

List not just who the product manager on the project is, but also the business analyst, lead developer, marketing lead, and so on. Anyone who has a say in the project should be listed here. If there is a project sponsor (a VP or C-level person), their name should be in here as well. This not only helps with communication, but also ensures that everyone who works on the project feels the weight of responsibility and ownership required to make good products.

Links

Most companies use tracking software to assign work to developers. This can be anything from heavy tools like Jira or Pivotal Tracker, to lighter ones like Trello or Basecamp. Sometimes other collaboration tools come into the mix as well (such as ConceptShare for providing feedback on graphic design), so it can become really difficult to keep everything together. Luckily most of these programs have URL schemes, which means you can gather all the entry points to the information in a central place — the links section of the functional spec. List here all implementation tickets, technical designs, visual assets, content, marketing communications, analytics requirements, and the rest. This will allow anyone to easily dive deep into any section of the project.

Problem Definition

Before any detail is shown, it's important to describe the problem that is being solved by the project. Everything comes back to this. If, two years down the line, a new VP comes on board and asks why your team did something (trust me, this *will* happen), the existence of this section in the spec will save you from a lot of heartache and re-work. It's astonishing how often companies reverse decisions or change the way they do things because they forget the reason why they did something in the first place. Don't let that happen to your projects.

Business Goals

It's essential to link the user goals identified in the problem definition to benefits for the business. What do you expect the impact to be on revenue, conversion rates, and so on? Include analytics and data on the current situation and expected change. This is where the three 'A's (acquisition, activation, activity) from chapter 6 can come in handy as well.

Success Metrics

How will you know the project was a success? It's important to set clear, measurable, attainable goals that everyone on the management and project teams agrees with. And don't forget to get the right benchmarks before any changes are made, so that progress can be measured accurately.

Competitive Analysis

If applicable, provide examples and analysis of competitor features or products that informed the project. It's important to be clear on this, not just to document ideas, but also because it keeps the team honest and focused on providing value that's distinctly different from how competitors do things.

Project Scope

This section is used not just to describe what is included in the project, but more importantly, to document what is out of scope. This is important because projects often spiral out of control (so-called feature creep), which can be avoided with a clear understanding of what systems or product areas are not planned to be changed in the project.

The project summary is the meta-information about the project. The purpose is to get everyone in the project team and beyond aligned on the goals and boundaries of the project, and also to build up organizational memory so that decisions don't get reversed in the future without proper reasoning and planning.

RISKS AND IMPACT ON OTHER PROJECTS

The next section of the spec takes a holistic view of the project by defining its impact on other projects and systems. It typically includes an outline of the following potential challenges:

- **Known risks**: what we should acknowledge as potential knock-on effects on other projects, such as contracts that need to be signed before anything can be implemented, services that need to be built to support new features, and so on.

- **Back-office impact**: the project's effect on out-of-sight areas that could be essential to successful execution. This includes finance, logistics, distribution, payments, and more.

- **Customer support impact**: is new help documentation needed? Do customer service agents need to be trained on any new or changed features? This is often an after-thought and can result in angry users and even angrier support agents.

- **Business intelligence impact**: what additional reporting is needed to ensure that the new product or features can be tracked effectively?

Once the summary and risks of the project have been outlined, it's time to get into the process of framing and describing the solution to the problem. Start broad, and then focus on specifics.

CUSTOMER JOURNEYS AND FLOW CHARTS

During the product discovery process you would have created customer journey maps, and possibly some personas. This is a visual summary of the problem as well as the solution, so it's a good idea to include those artifacts in the spec since they provide additional context on how the project fits into the larger vision.

Customer journey map (Larger view[106])

This is also a good place to include any flow diagrams that will help developers and testers complete their technical designs and QA plans. This is especially true if there is complex logic that dictates the different paths users can take through a flow. Most will be familiar with the classic boxes and arrows format for flow charts, which looks something like this:

---

106. http://smashed.by/customer-journey-map

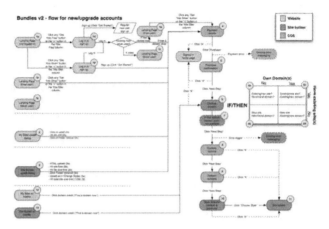

Example of a flow chart (Larger view[107])

That format definitely works well, but I've also started to use what Ryan Singer from Basecamp calls "flow shorthand" diagrams[108]:

WHAT THE
USER SEES
→
WHAT THEY
SEE NEXT

WHAT THEY
DO

WHAT THEY
DO NEXT

Here's an example of what it looks like when completed:

---

107. http://smashed.by/flow-chart
108. "A shorthand for designing UI flows" – http://smashed.by/ui-flows

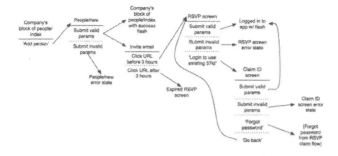

Source for both images: Ryan Singer[109]

This approach is particularly useful because it accounts very specifically for so-called red paths[110] — those parts of a flow where users can get stuck or make mistakes. Identifying the red paths in a flow early on helps in two ways.

First, it forces designers to think about designing for error prevention. If you know where a user might go wrong, it's possible to design a flow that prevents them from making that mistake. A simple example is the practice of only showing a *Next* or *Continue* button once all required fields in a form have been filled out. This avoids the need to present error messages on form submission, since the form can't be submitted until all fields have been completed.

Second, red paths force us to think through error handling as well. I always think about error handling as the bastard child of user experience design. No one thinks about it until it's too late, and then they try to sweep it un-

---

109. http://smashed.by/ui-flows
110. Red being the color of danger, of course.

der the rug. But good error handling — inline validation, messaging that is clear and helpful — provides essential microinteractions in a good interface.

SKETCHES, WIREFRAMES AND PROTOTYPES

The UX industry is slowly moving away from using static wireframes in UI design, and in most cases that's a good thing. Static wireframes are helpful to communicate a concept, but they usually require too much effort for the payoff, since there are faster ways to communicate ideas (sketching), and better ways to test the validity of those concepts (interactive prototypes).

So, in most cases, this section of the spec will include some photos of the sketching process to show early ideas — especially what different kinds of ideas were explored before settling on a direction. Variation versus iteration, remember?

It then usually also includes a link to an interactive prototype, built in software like Axure, or frameworks like Bootstrap or Foundation. The prototype is often the part of the spec that's most referenced by developers, since it's the most useful. Instead of having to read through documents, or asking someone a question every time they encounter a new interface element, prototypes allow them to just click around and figure out what the intention is (and ask someone if it's not clear).

The spec usually points to the final version of the prototype, but it's also good to include links and references to earlier versions that were used for customer validation. As discussed in an chapter 6, the prototyping phase is a hypothesis phase, where different ideas are tested with real users, and changes are made based on that feedback.

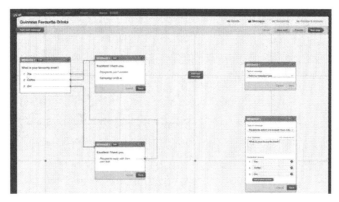

Example of a page from an Axure prototype (Larger view[111])

GRAPHIC DESIGN

This part of the spec communicates the visual direction of the product. This can take a variety of formats. As mentioned before, I don't agree completely that we're entering a post-PSD era, but I do believe we're in a reduced-PSD era, where we don't need to create PSD files for every page or screen in the product.

Instead, a combination of a good interactive prototype, style tiles[112], and a few key PSD files, are more than enough for developers to code up the pages. Style tiles are particularly useful because they separate the discussion of what the interface looks like ("I don't like yellow!") from the discussion of how it works ("That button is in

111. http://smashed.by/axure-prototype
112. http://styletil.es

the wrong place"). In my experience, if arguments about the prototype and the visual direction happen separately, it's much easier to move from prototype to the graphic design and development phases, because most of the issues of look and feel have already been worked through.

The level of graphic design provided in the spec depends entirely on the nature of the business, and how designers and developers prefer to work together (more on that later). For some organizations, annotated PSDs work well; others want each element cut up and described in detail; while some developers are happy to dig around in the PSD files and create a UI component library[113] based on what they find there. There is no single right way, but it's important that everyone has input on what those deliverables are.

THE LAST TWENTY PERCENT

With all these sections in place, you should have a functional spec that not only provides the background and context for the project and the user and business goals you're hoping to solve, but is also a document that is actually used during development. Imagine that! But there are a couple final points that are important to make about functional specs.

First, this isn't a document that the PM writes the day before development starts. This is a document that is be-

---

113. Component libraries are beyond the scope of this book, but this is a great way to define visual standards for a product. For more background on this approach, see "How and why to create a pattern library" by Paul Boag: http://smashed.by/pattern-library

gun as soon as a new project kicks off. I always create a template in our wiki (or wherever the plan is to store specs), and open it up as soon I start work on a new project. The best way to write a spec like this is to add information to it as it becomes available. So I add the customer journey map as soon as we complete it. I add the sketches right after the design studio session. This reinforces that idea that the spec is a living document open to collaboration, and it also breaks up the workload so that it doesn't feel like a huge effort to create it.

Second, remember to pick only what you need from this list — nothing more. For some smaller projects I skip the customer journey and prototyping phase, and move straight from sketching changes to development. That's OK. Don't think of the sections above as law; think of them as an à la carte menu that you can pick and choose from based on the needs of the project.

And finally, remember that functional specs will only get you about eighty percent of the way to shipping. The last twenty percent of product definition happens during development. That's how it should be. The spec provides the background and proposed direction, but it's only when you start walking on the path that you will discover the rocks in the way that need to be moved and avoided. Embrace that, and get comfortable with negotiating with designers and developers to find good trade-offs. Want to avoid using JavaScript on a page, but that means you'll have to absolutely position an element on a page, which has unintended design consequences? Well, that's a trade-off between progressive enhancement and design idealism. The role of product manager is to understand that trade-off, listen to each side's argument, and then make a call and move on (and remember — live with the consequences).

Some people roll their eyes at functional specifications, believing it's part of old-school product management that isn't relevant any more. But I'll repeat what I said earlier: specs aren't bad — bad specs are bad. If you create documentation people actually use to build the product and understand why certain decisions were made, how can you argue that it's not useful? So don't stop writing specs. Just start writing really good ones.

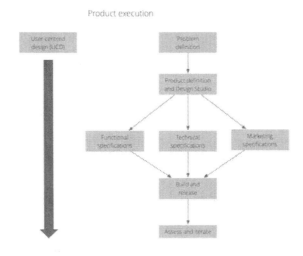

Let's just take a moment to remind ourselves where we are in the product execution process. We've now discussed problem and product definition, and after a detour into user-centered design we talked about the importance of functional specifications. So now we're going to discuss the other types of specifications that are also important: technical, and marketing.

Technical Specifications

Whereas the functional specification describes how a product works from a user's perspective, the technical specification describes how the product will be implemented. It describes things like data structures and database models, and what programming languages and frameworks will be used. The technical spec is usually not written by the product manager, but by the technical lead on the project.

In general, technical specifications should:

- Reiterate the user and business goals as laid out in the functional specification.

- Define the system architecture and infrastructure.

- Define the background tasks required to enable the defined user flows.

- Define the database model.

- Define the interfaces to other back-office systems.

- Define the non-functional requirements (list things like desired page size, response times, and so on).

Product managers who come from non-technical backgrounds are often less inclined to get involved in this part of the project. Although I don't believe it's essential for product managers to know how to code, it is important for them to understand enough of the technological architecture and infrastructure to help guide technical specifications. In some cases, additional programming might be necessary to support a feature in the way it was designed. It is then the PM's role to understand all the trade-offs involved. Does the extra work required result in a significant usability improvement, or can the same goal be accomplished through a slightly easier implementation?

The PM might not write the technical spec, but they know it inside out.

Marketing Specifications

The marketing team's involvement in product development is a touchy subject. There is often quite a disconnect between what product designers and marketing team members find important. The marketing team is focused on how to sell a product to users, whereas product designers are focused on making a product that is so good that it won't need any fancy sales tactics. The reality is that these groups have to meet in the middle, because they need each other. Marketing can't sell a bad product effectively, and product designers have to learn how to communicate the benefits of their products to users.

To ensure the marketing team and product team work well together, the marketing team has to be involved at appropriate phases of the development process. And the development of marketing requirements is the perfect place for collaboration. Marketing requirements specify who the users are for a particular product, and what benefits should be used to sell the product to those users.

The structure I like most for marketing requirements is one that Amazon uses frequently: writing a short internal press release (no more than two pages) before any design or development starts. This press release stays inside the company, and doesn't go to any media outlets. Instead, it is used to help internal marketing teams understand what the product is about, and as an added bonus it also helps to keep product teams focused. Ian McAllister explains[114]:

> Internal press releases are centered around the customer problem, how current solutions (internal or external) fail, and how the new product will blow away existing solutions.

When PMs collaborate with the marketing team on a press release before the product is released, they are completely aligned on who and what the product is for, and how it will be sold to users. If anything happens during the development phase to change a product so that it's no longer in line with the press release, that's a good time to pause and figure out what needs to change: the press release, or the planned feature change?

Keeping marketing requirements in sync with functional and technical requirements throughout the development process not only helps to build healthy relation-

---

114. Ian McAllister's answer to "What is Amazon's approach to product development and product management?" – http://smashed.by/mcallister-amzn

ships with the marketing team, but it's also another check to ensure that you're only building products and features that meet actual user and business goals.

McAllister recommends the following sections in the internal press release, which aligns very well with the process we've outlined so far:

- **Heading:** *Name the product in a way the reader (i.e. your target customers) will understand.*

- **Sub-Heading:** *Describe who the market for the product is and what benefit they get. One sentence only underneath the title.*

- **Summary:** *Give a summary of the product and the benefit. Assume the reader will not read anything else so make this paragraph good.*

- **Problem:** *Describe the problem your product solves.*

- **Solution:** *Describe how your product elegantly solves the problem.*

- **Quote from You:** *A quote from a spokesperson in your company.*

- **How to Get Started:** *Describe how easy it is to get started.*

- **Customer Quote:** *Provide a quote from a hypothetical customer that describes how they experienced the benefit.*

- **Closing and Call to Action:** *Wrap it up and give pointers where the reader should go next.*

With these three flexible documents in place, it's time to start the development phase and get the product built. ❧

CHAPTER 8:

Build And Release

When it's time to start development, most of the building blocks for a successful development cycle should already be in place. You'll have clearly defined problem definitions and goals, and you'll have living functional, technical, and marketing specifications that clearly define what the product is about while still providing room for change and improvisation. You'll have a roadmap that doesn't specify timelines and release dates, but clearly shows the priority of what issues are being worked on in any given cycle. So getting the thing shipped will be easy, right?

Well, not so fast. We all know how crazy things can get during development, and how quickly the finger-pointing starts when something goes wrong. The truth is that most people are scared to work with developers, and that affects the quality of the output because there are so many misunderstandings along the way. But it's not necessary to be scared of developers! It's just extremely important to understand how developers work most effectively. The good news is, as Jeff Ello points out[115]:

> Unlike in many industries, the fight in most IT groups is in how to get things done, not how to avoid work. IT pros will self-organize, disrupt and subvert in the name of accomplishing work.

---

115. "The unspoken truth about managing geeks" – http://smashed.by/ managing-geeks

Once you understand this, you also start to realize that developers don't hate process. They hate process that doesn't help them get things done. So they react very strongly to things like useless fifteen-person meetings and forty-page Word documents.

To solve this problem, the needs of makers (such as designers and developers) should be taken seriously by managers (those who direct and enable the work). It is the product manager's job to make sure that everyone in the organization understands makers' work, and also to define the rules of engagement with developers to protect their time. Mike Monteiro takes on this issue by attacking the humble calendar in "The Chokehold of Calendars[116]":

> *Meetings may be toxic, but calendars are the superfund sites that allow that toxicity to thrive. All calendars suck. And they all suck in the same way. Calendars are a record of interruptions. And quite often they're a battlefield over who owns whose time.*

Paul Graham takes a more holistic view in "Maker's Schedule, Manager's Schedule[117]." He explains that managers break their days up into hour-long stretches of time, while makers need large blocks of time in order to focus:

> *When you're operating on the maker's schedule, meetings are a disaster. A single meeting can blow a whole af-*

---

116. "The Chokehold of Calendars" – http://smashed.by/calendars
117. "Maker's Schedule, Manager's Schedule" – http://smashed.by/makers-schedule

ternoon, by breaking it into two pieces, each too small to do anything hard in. Plus you have to remember to go to the meeting. That's no problem for someone on the manager's schedule. There's always something coming on the next hour; the only question is what. But when someone on the maker's schedule has a meeting, they have to think about it.

Makers need long stretches of uninterrupted time to get things done, and get them done well. Most corporate environments don't support this because of an insatiable need for everyone to agree on everything. So helping people understand why this is such a big deal for makers is important, so that then you can effect cultural change.

Michael Lopp talks about this in his article "Managing Nerds[118]." Substitute the word "nerds" in this article with "designers and developers" (no offense intended). Michael describes how nerds are forever chasing two highs.

The first high is unraveling the knot: that moment when they figure out how to solve a particular problem ("Finally, a simple way to get users through this flow."). But the second high is more important. This is when "complete knot domination" takes place — when they step away from the ten unraveled knots, understand what created the knots, and set their minds to making sure the knots don't happen again ("OK, let's build a UI component that can be used whenever this situation occurs.").

---

118. "Managing Nerds" – http://smashed.by/managing-nerds

Chasing the Second High is where nerds earn their salary. If the First High is the joy of understanding, the Second High is the act of creation. If you want your nerd to rock your world by building something revolutionary, you want them chasing the Second High.

And the way to help designers and developers chase the second high is to "obsessively protect both [their] time and space":

The almost-constant quest of the nerd is managing all the crap that is preventing us from entering the Zone as we search for the Highs.

So, how do you change a culture built around meetings and interruptions? How do you understand what designers and developers need in order to be effective, and how do you relentlessly protect them from distractions? Here are a few ways to start.

Ask The Makers

Find out what designers and developers need, and then make it happen. A quiet corner to work in? Sure. A bigger screen? Absolutely. No interruptions while the headphones are on? Totally fine. Whatever it takes to help them be as creative as possible and to be free to chase that second high.

Also ask developers how they would like to be included in the product development process. Some might prefer to stay in their quiet corners and just code. But there are also some who would jump at the opportunity to be involved all along the process—from concept and design all the way through release. The earlier PMs bring developers into the process, the better. Their ideas and input are invaluable, and they can also point out possible constraints early enough in the project to save a lot of pain and rework down the road.

Start Working On A Better Meeting Culture

This one is a constant struggle for organizations of all sizes, and there are many ways to address it. I try to adhere to two simple rules. First, a meeting has to produce something: a sketch, a research plan, a technical design, a strategic decision to change the roadmap, and so on. Second, no large status meetings to update the management team on what's going on. That's what Google Docs and wikis are for.

I wouldn't go so far as to say that meetings are toxic[119], but the need to have an agenda and a tangible outcome should go without saying. I also like Scott Berkun's proposal to deal with recurring meetings[120]:

> Even back at Microsoft I had this rule about recurring meetings: at meeting birth, it should be planned that they will die. They will stop being useful at some point. But many of us suffer through zombie meetings, that live on in an undead state forever. Often there is one per-

119. See "Meetings Are Toxic" by 37signals – http://smashed.by/meetings
120. "Do You Need That Meeting?" – http://smashed.by/need-that-meeting

*son who feels powerful in the meeting, and they will
keep feeding the zombie with the coworker's brains just
to preserve that feeling.*

Meetings should focus on facilitating the things that
meetings are good at: collective thinking. Meetings that
energize me are the ones where most people are standing,
working together on a common goal. From customer
journey workshops to design studio sessions to analyzing
usability testing results, there are plenty of useful ways
to spend our times in meetings. So, death to zombie meetings. Life to meetings that make products better.

Help Designers And Developers Understand One Another

Lucas Rocha talks about the importance of designers and
developers working closely together in "Mind the Gap[121]":

*Iterative design processes that engage designers and engineers very early tend to result in higher UI quality because it provides the necessary flexibility and agility to
steer ideas as they are implemented. Sounds obvious but
this is much easier said than done. Just see how rare [it]
is to find products with outstanding user interfaces.*

This is very true, and the power of small, collaborative
teams has been proven time and again. But it's important
to take this further. It's not just about collaboration, it's

---

121. "Mind the Gap" – http://smashed.by/mind-the-gap

also about empathy. If designers and developers collaborate but don't understand one another, you'll still get nowhere.

The main issue is that designers and developers approach their respective crafts from very different perspectives. Design is about composition—how to put hundreds of tiny elements together so that the whole makes sense. Development is about deconstruction—how to break down the whole into pieces that can be implemented effectively. That creates a disconnect that is difficult to overcome if there isn't empathy between the two groups.

Thomas Petersen describes the ideal situation really well in "Developers are from Mars, Designers from Venus[122]":

> They are the developers who can design enough to appreciate what good design can do for their product even if it sometimes means having to deviate from the framework and put a little extra effort into customizing certain functionality. [...]
>
> And they are the designers who learn how to think like a programmer when they design and develop an aesthetic that is better suited for deconstruction rather than composition.

So, it's not just about meeting more often. It's also about meeting in the middle to accomplish a common goal together.

---

122. "Developers are from Mars, Designers from Venus — A question of metaphors" – http://smashed.by/mars-venus

Celebrate Successes

Dhanji R. Prasanna was a developer on Google Wave, and when he left Google he wrote an excellent post on some of the issues with working in big companies. In "The Mythical Man-Month[123]" he wrote:

> [A]s a programmer you must have a series of wins, every single day. [...] It is what makes you eager for the next feature, and the next after that. And a large team is poison to small wins. The nature of large teams is such that even when you do have wins, they come after long, tiresome and disproportionately many hurdles. And this takes all the wind out of them. Often when I shipped a feature it felt more like relief than euphoria.

It's so important for large teams to celebrate success with the people they work with every day. It is hard to get that right in large organizations because the invisibility of individual team members and the pressures to move on to The Next Thing aren't naturally conducive to this type of behavior. But it's possible if you work at it.

Whether you keep some champagne in a fridge, send out company-wide emails thanking people by name, or ring a bell every time code gets deployed (OK, that last one is lame, sorry), being in a large organization isn't an excuse for acting like a faceless corporation.

One more thing: remember that release day is a big deal. As the product manager, you are the conductor on release day. Be at the office (or in the chat room) first, and

---

123. "The Mythical Man-Month" – http://smashed.by/mmm

leave last. Make sure everyone has what they need, and make your one goal be helping things go smoothly. And don't forget the champagne. The team deserves a win, so make a big deal out of it when the project is live—even if you have a release every two weeks.

One of the most important jobs of a product manager is to show progress in the product, because this motivates the team and shows users that you are listening and invested. So don't just plan a bunch of projects. Ship them. As often as possible. ❧

CHAPTER 9:

Assess And Iterate

Earlier in the book we discussed the importance of defining success metrics before any changes are made to a product — and making sure there are benchmarks against which you can measure that success. I also talked about the three 'A's, which can be quite useful to help identify the most appropriate metrics: acquisition, activation, and activity.

Once the project is live it's time for the reckoning. This is what it all leads up to for a product manager: finding out if all the hard work paid off, or if you'll have to make some changes to get where you need to be. This feedback loop is important because it not only determines success, it also helps you figure out what areas to focus on next.

When I was in primary school one of my favorite statistics was (somewhat morbidly) related to car accidents. Once I'd heard that most car accidents happen close to home[124], I couldn't stop sharing that fact everywhere I went. "It's obvious," I would go on, "that people don't pay as much attention to their driving when they're almost home." It was only later that I realized the reason most car accidents happen close to home is because most driving happens close to home. I always think about that story as my first exposure to the danger of data, and how easily we jump to conclusions on a single data point. This

---

124. "One in three road accidents happen a mile from home, survey says", Daily Telegraph, August 13, 2009 – http://smashed.by/accidents

is why it's so important for the assessment process to include both qualitative and quantitative measures.

Research triangulation — also known as mixed method research — is a helpful methodology to keep in mind here. Research triangulation is the process of combining several research methods to study a single phenomenon (or in this case, the effects of a single project). This ensures that each method is balanced out so that, for example, you're not placing too much weight on analytics while ignoring survey or usability testing feedback. I usually like using a balance of three research method to determine success.

1. WEB ANALYTICS

Measure the pre- and post-launch metrics with Google Analytics, ClickTale, or your preferred analytics provider. This is the hard data, the numbers, the thing that ultimately counts for business success. However, it's not the whole story.

2. ONLINE SURVEYS

When I worked at eBay I ran a program called Product Tracker, which involved running a series of surveys every quarter, asking the same questions, to measure how sentiments about each of our flows changed over time. This way we could see how the analytics corresponded to attitudes and feelings about the product.

3. USABILITY TESTING

As I keep mentioning, analytics (and surveys too) are good at showing you what is happening, but you need a qualitative method like usability testing to understand why something is happening. This is the only way to find out why something works (do more of this!) or doesn't work (do this differently!).

In an impassioned plea to designers and developers at a meetup in August 2013, Stijn Debrouwere explained how our obsession with analytics only (without other pieces of data) can be really detrimental to the product development process. Speaking specifically about the publishing industry, Stijn said[125]:

> *Pageviews is a vanity metric: something that looks really important but that we can't act on and that tell us nothing about how well we're actually doing, financially or otherwise.*
>
> *[…]*
>
> *There's nothing like a dashboard full of data and graphs and trend lines to make us feel like grown ups. Like people who know what they're doing. So even though we're not getting any real use out of it, it's addictive and we can't stop doing it.*

This is not to say analytics are not useful. But we have to define exactly what we're measuring, and how that will help us make a better product. And then we have to triangulate those results with other methods to make it truly useful.

There is a big culture of A/B testing, or test and learn, in the software development community. But even

---

125. "Cargo cult analytics" – http://smashed.by/cargo-cult

though A/B testing can be extremely valuable to help identify the best iteration of a site or a particular page, it should never be used in isolation.

Since A/B testing is relatively cheap to do and the results are so compelling, companies are in danger of adopting a test and learn culture where pages are just A/B tested with no additional user input. That would be the wrong way to go. A/B testing shouldn't be used on its own to make decisions — it should always be used in conjunction with other research methods, both qualitative (such as usability testing and ethnography) and quantitative (such as desirability studies).

A/B testing is an important method in the research toolkit because it can give you information that usability testing on its own cannot. The main goal of A/B testing is to see how business metrics move up and down depending on the version of the page — click-through rates, checkout rates, purchasing rates, and so on. You can't see that with usability testing alone. But as Kohavi et al point out in their paper "Practical Guide to Controlled Experiments on the Web[126]", A/B testing has some major limitations:

- "Short term versus long term effects." Since A/B testing methods generally use controlled experiments that run for a few days or weeks, some long-term effects — such as users becoming familiar with a new design and eventual-

---

126. Ron Kohavi, Roger Longbotham, Dan Sommerfield, Randal M. Henne; "Practical Guide to Controlled Experiments on the Web: Listen to Your Customers not to the HiPPO," *Data Mining and Knowledge Discovery*, February 2009, Volume 18, Issue 1, pp 140-181.

ly preferring it — aren't accounted for. This is another reason to follow up with additional quantitative and qualitative research a few months after a change was made based on A/B testing data.

- "Primacy and newness effects." These issues represent two sides of the same coin. A primacy effect can be observed when a change to a familiar pattern causes experienced users to be uncertain and hesitate. A new feature, on the other hand, can encourage some users to concentrate all their attention on it. Such issues suggest that A/B testing should be run several times over a longer period, or recruit only new users who won't be subject to the influence of these effects.

- "Features must be implemented." Sometimes the feature being tested is not fully developed, since it's seen as a test. This can bias the data: if the feature doesn't perform well it might be due to poor execution, not because the feature itself is ineffective.

- "Consistency." Because of the way most A/B testing platforms work, it's possible for users to see different versions of the same page on different computers. This can cause confusion for users and further bias the data.

The point of raising these concerns is not to say that we shouldn't use A/B testing, but that it is important to use testing responsibly. Since every research and testing method comes with its own limitations, a combination of methods is the only way to get the full picture and make the right decisions.

A common example of how single-source metrics can be confusing is time on site, a metric that most sites track religiously. The problem here is that it's very difficult to know if the goal should be to increase or decrease time on site. If a user spends more time on a site, is it because they're more engaged, or because they can't figure out what to do? If they spend less time on a site, is it because they're bored, or because they were able to accomplish their task very quickly? The metrics can tell us that something has changed, but we need qualitative methods to understand why those changes happen.

It's essential to take what you learn back into the product development process. So everything you learn here feeds back into the gathering of user, business, and technical needs that started it all. And on and on the cycle goes: release, learn, improve. That's what being a product manager is all about. ✌

CHAPTER 10:

Product Management In Agile Methodologies

Throughout the book I've deliberately avoided talking about specific development methodologies like agile or waterfall. Product management is a discipline that sits apart from any specific methodology. These are universal skills and methods that can be applied regardless of the philosophy a company uses to build software. But since agile techniques are currently the most common way companies choose to implement their projects, I wanted to touch on it briefly. I'm not going to spend much time discussing the mechanics of agile development — there are other texts much better suited for that. This definition from Anthony Colfelt[127] will suffice for our purposes:

> *Agile is an iterative development approach that takes small steps toward defining a product or service.*

Because of its iterative approach, agile methods fit the lean model very well, and the process has several important benefits:

• Quicker return on development investment.

• Constant feedback to help improve the product.

---

127. "Bringing User Centered Design to the Agile Environment" – http://smashed.by/agile

- It generates product momentum, which is good for users as well as development teams.

- It encourages contributions from different perspectives since it relies heavily on cross-functional teams.

But there are also quite a few challenges to overcome, as Colfelt points out:

- **An unclear role for design.** We haven't quite figured out how to incorporate UX into the agile environment. There are some good approaches, but we're all still trying to get there.

- **The product discovery process is not well defined.** Agile techniques focus on iteration, which means there is rarely time for defining a problem properly, and trying out a few solutions before picking the iteration to go for.

- **The temptation to call it "good enough."** Shipping beats perfection in agile, which is great, but it can be taken too far. Quality can start falling by the wayside completely in the interest of keeping up velocity, and that is really bad for the product.

The important point to remember is that agile methodologies are good for *refining* a product, but not good for *defining* a product. To use language we've relied on throughout the book, agile is for iteration, not variation. Scott Sehlhorst also pointed out one of the biggest dangers of agile in "The One Idea of Your Product[128]":

Agile is not a process by which you start typing without any idea of what you intend, releasing it and then getting feedback in an iterative process. If that's how you're approaching agile, your process is broken.

This means that the product manager fulfills a crucial role in the agile environment, primarily to ensure that there is enough variation in the product design process, not just iteration, and that there is a clear plan and vision. In particular, here are some things to remember for product managers in an agile environment.

- **The product manager is the product owner**
  In agile teams, the product manager fulfills the role of product owner. This might seem obvious, but sometimes teams bring product owners in who don't have a background in some of the other aspects we've discussed in this book, like planning and strategy. This is dangerous because...

- **Product ownership is a role within the larger responsibilities of the product manager**
  One of the issues I see in the agile community is that the titles "product manager" and "product owner" are often used interchangeably. This is a problem because it has the potential to confuse teams into thinking that the only activities product owners are responsible for are those that are officially part of the agile methodology, such as backlog grooming.

---

128. "The One Idea of Your Product" – http://smashed.by/one-idea

- **You still have to plan ahead**
  Being agile doesn't mean you can just stumble along and
  hope it all works out. There's no use shipping workable
  software if it's software that no one wants to use. That's
  not failing fast, that's taking on unnecessary risk. Product
  vision and roadmaps are still important in an agile environment.

- **Try to be one or two sprints ahead of the team**
  There is certainly some disagreement about the idea of
  sprint zero, and always making sure that design and
  product are a little bit ahead of the team. But I've found
  that making sure all the UX ducks are in a row — at least
  eighty percent of the way — before a sprint starts is the
  only way to make sure that core principles of utility and
  usability don't get thrown out in the interest of delivering
  a product as quickly as possible.

- **Replace heavy specs with right-fidelity specifications**
  Light prototypes, documented as outlined in chapter 7 on
  specifications, is the right way to go with agile as well.

- **Follow the spirit of agile, not the letter**
  It's very easy to get caught up in the rules of agile. I've
  seen people make a religion out of backlog grooming,
  sprint planning, retrospectives, and so on. The spirit of
  agile is to iterate and learn your way to better software.
  The process helps you get there, but it's OK to ignore or
  change the parts that don't work for the team.

  Below is a diagram that shows one approach to include
  product and UX work in a typical scrum environment:

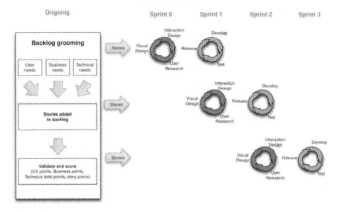

UX and Scrum

An approach to integrating design and scrum principles (Larger view[129])

Stories are added to the backlog based on the user needs, business needs, and technical needs that are uncovered during regular product planning. So far, so good. The part that's particularly important from a product management perspective is to not just use story points to score each story. The user, business, and technical needs must have a huge impact on the priority of stories, so each story should also be scored based on those aspects.

From the prioritized backlog, I've still experienced that the most effective way to keep the design team involved throughout the delivery process is to make sure design and prototype testing happen a sprint or two before each of the delivery steps. In this way the generic model for

---

129. http://smashed.by/ux-and-scrum

product management I shared in this book can still be applied effectively to agile development. ✌

CHAPTER 11:

Getting Started

The last chapter of a book like this usually contains a summary. But that doesn't feel right for a topic that's all about doing. So instead, I want to address a different topic for this chapter, a question I hear all the time: where do I start? The theory is nice, the framework is nice, but how do you actually jump in, and start being a product manager? As it turns out, this makes for a good summary of the book anyway, so it's a win-win situation.

Arriving at a company as a new (or sometimes, the first) product manager can be daunting. Product management is usually introduced in an organization once there is such a high level of internal enthusiasm and chaos that the leaders aren't sure how to handle it any more. And then everyone looks to the product manager to "manage stuff."

It's easy to get overwhelmed by how much there is to do when you step into a stressful role like product management. So here are some recommendations on how to spend your first three months at a new company.

First 30 Days

UNDERSTAND THE PRODUCT, THE MARKET, AND THE COMPANY CULTURE

Here's how I defined product management in chapter 1:

The product manager's mission is to achieve business success by meeting user needs through the continuous planning and execution of digital product solutions.

With that in mind, spend the first thirty days learning and understanding:

- **The product**
  What does the company sell? What does the product do? How does it work? What is the value proposition? What problems does it solve for customers? What features does it have? What kind of bugs does it have? What are the main usability issues?

- **The market**
  Who currently uses the product? What are they like? What are their characteristics? What do they like and not like about the product? Who is the target market? Are there personas for each different type of person in the target market? What are macro- and micro-market needs addressed by the product? Who are the competitors?

- **The current product/market fit**
  Are you in a good market with a product that can satisfy the market? What are the gaps you need to close between what the product does, and what the market needs, to ensure a better fit?

- **The company culture**
  Talk to as many people as possible in the organization — from marketing to finance to design to engineering — to understand how things work. What do people like about the product development process? What do

they hate? Do designers feel like they have enough time to do their work? Do developers have what they need to program effectively?

Above all, ensure the PM role is properly understood by everyone. As we discussed earlier, for a product manager to be effective, the organization needs to understand that PMs should have autonomy over the products they manage. Executive buy-in is a prerequisite for success, so make sure it's well understood that even though everyone gets a voice, not everyone gets to decide. Remember Seth Godin's words: "Nothing is what happens when everyone has to agree."

Next 30 Days

DEVELOP A STRATEGIC PRODUCT PLAN

Based on what you learn in the first thirty days, start the product planning phase:

- Run a **product discovery workshop** to start identifying user needs, business needs, and technical needs, and to create a problem frame diagram.

- Develop **personas and customer journeys**, and start brainstorming ideas for product development with the team.

- Work with the team to **prioritize ideas and start building a roadmap** for development. Consider methods like the KJ-Method or the Kano model as a way to formalize prioritization efforts.

- **Identify success measures** — define how you'll know if what you're doing is having the desired impact. The three 'A's (acquisition, activation, activity) are always a good start.

- Put the **appropriate processes** in place to ensure effective product development life cycles. This means knowing what kind of specifications developers need to start working, how research and design fits into the process, how to ensure hypothesis and prototype testing is baked into the way you work, where marketing becomes involved, how QA should work, and so on. You can only do this once you understand the current culture, and what the strategic plan will be.

All of the above goes into the strategic product plan, as we defined it earlier. Among other things, this plan includes statements about the product's value proposition, who the market is (customer profiles), how you plan to achieve product/market fit (the business opportunity, pricing, distribution), what the priorities are, a first stab at the roadmap, and proposed success measures.

Final 30 Days

Now that the plan and the initial roadmap are in place,
start the product execution phase:

- **Start with a reasonably small problem definition** with
  clear and easily measurable success metrics. Work with
  the team to get it done right (collaborative teamwork,
  constant learning through prototype testing, right-fidelity specifications).

- **Measure, and show the success of the process.** Use
  this to build trust and continue to ship improvements
  (and even better products).

- **Assess** the situation, and use customer and business
  feedback to adjust priorities (and the roadmap) as needed.
  Flexibility is key.

- **Keep going.** Repeat any of the initial steps as needed.

- **Have fun** while you're doing all of this.

After the first ninety days, use the framework I discussed
in this book to get into the rhythm of building great products: constant learning, constant testing, constant dreaming, constant building. There will never be a dull moment.

What I've shown in this book is that the life of a product manager has an exhausting, exhilarating rhythm that
is as invigorating as it is excruciating. Spending your

time systematically moving from product planning to product execution, and moving between those phases seamlessly, will not only give you a solid foundation from which to improve the product, but also ensure that you ship the right improvements at the right time.

There are thousands of ways to make a living. But we, the product managers, choose to spend our time dreaming up products and getting them out into the world. That is an incredible privilege, and an opportunity I wouldn't trade for anything. We get to work on understanding people, and finding out how technology can improve their lives. Yes, it's stressful, but it is so, so worth it. Let's go make the best products we can possibly make, together. ❧

Acknowledgements

None of this would have happened if Francisco Inchauste didn't discover my blog (I still don't know how) and decided to take a chance on me. Because of him I started writing for Smashing Magazine. Because of that work I built up a relationship with Vitaly. And that gave me the opportunity to pitch this book idea. I'm also incredibly grateful that he agreed to be the technical editor for the book. He played equal parts editor and psychologist, which is exactly what I needed. Francisco, I am forever in your debt. Thank you.

Vitaly Friedman, Markus Seyfferth, and the rest of the Smashing Magazine team took this project on with open arms, and I'm so thankful for that. They're such a friendly, passionate crew, and a joy to work with. Thank you for your dedication and support throughout this project.

Owen Gregory came in at just the right moment to do much more than copyediting. He asked critical questions that ironed out some of the issues I just couldn't see before because I was too close to the text. Thanks, Owen, you're awesome.

I love the illustrations Anna Shuvalova made for the book. It's pretty much what I saw in my head. Thanks Anna!

Speaking of what's in my head, Francisco also did the cover design, and he did such an amazing job. I want this design on a T-shirt and wear it all the time, but I guess that would be going a little overboard.

Last but not least, thank you to my wife Jessica and my two wonderful daughters Aralyn and Emery. They endured lots of stress and Saturday morning coffee shop sessions to get this thing done. None of this matters without them, so this is their book. Don't worry guys, you don't have to read it. I just want to dedicate it to you. ❧

About The Author

Rian van der Merwe is passionate about designing and building software that people love to use. After spending several years working in Silicon Valley and Cape Town, he is currently based in Portland, OR. He blogs[130] and tweets[131] regularly about user experience and product management.

---

130. http://www.elezea.com/
131. http://twitter.com/rianvdm

Made in the USA
San Bernardino, CA
11 February 2016